ALL ABOUT

UCP 600

(Uniform Customs and Practice for Documentary Credits, International Chamber of Commerce, Paris, Publication No 600)

(Second edition)

The transition from UCP 500 and the critical issues in between.

Rupnarayan Bose

All About UCP 600

Date of publication: April 2023

ISBN: Please see back cover

Publisher: Independently published

Cover design: Siddhartha Bose

While every effort has been made to avoid mistakes or omissions, this publication is being sold on the condition and understanding that neither the author nor the publishers or printers would be liable in any manner to any person by reason of any mistake or omission in this publication or for any action taken or omitted to be taken or advice rendered or accepted on the basis of this work. For any defect in printing or binding the publishers will be liable only to replace the defective copy by another copy of this work when available.

ALL ABOUT UCP 600

CONTENTS

By the same author:

- The ABCs of container shipment (April 2022)
- Understanding Trade Finance through Q&A and Case Studies Notion Press (April 2022)
- *Beyond Trade Finance*, Notion Press (April 2021)
- *Letters of Credit: Theory and Practice,* Notion Press (April 2020)
- *A complete guide to letters of credit and the UCP*, Laxmi Publications,
- *All About UCP 600 (1st edition),* Macmillan India Limited, 2007
- *Fundamentals of International Banking (1st edition),* Macmillan India Limited, 2007 (under revision)
- *An Introduction to Documentary Credits*, Macmillan India Limited, 2006

******

Copyright acknowledgement:

PREFACE TO THE SECOND EDITION

All of us have come a long way since the UCP 2007 version was published by the International Chamber of Commerce (ICC), Paris. Since then, ICC came out with several other publications covering a wide spectrum of international trade. However, UCP 600 continues as the mainstay of documentary credit operations worldwide.

The Foreword to the first edition is reproduced in this book. It provides to the reader the background to this work and to the evolution of the UCP to its latest version.

This edition updates the information in the earlier edition, removes data that has become obsolete, and presents a leaner and a more precise version of the previous edition.

I am sure everyone will appreciate the background information about the UCP – especially the perspective that this book helps to present to the discerning reader – about how the 2007 version of the UCP came to be, how its articles took shape, the issues considered and debated before being accepted or rejected, why certain articles in UCP 600 are the way they are and so on. The information in this book will help the reader to gain a better understanding of the UCP as a whole. An important fact that is sure to impress a reader is the wide-ranging issues that the Drafting Group had to address and find a solution to, issues that some of us take for granted while going through UCP 600.

A few words about the ISBP – International Standard Banking Practice for the Examination of Documents under Documentary Credits (UCP 600). ISBP 645 was replaced by ISBP, ICC Publication No. 681 with effect from 01 July 2007. However, since ISBP, ICC Publication No. 645 was in operation throughout the period covered by the revision process (ISBP 681 coming into being much later), most of the reference to the ISBP in this book are to Publication No. 645, unless specifically stated otherwise. Since ISBP 745 was published much after the release of UCP 600, several *rules* that should have found a place in the UCP were accommodated – unfortunately, in the opinion of this author – in the ISBP itself in the guise of procedures or clarifications, not in the UCP by way of "rules" as these ought to have been.

Reference to the currently operative version of the ISBP (ICC ISBP 745) is shown wherever possible.

One hopes that someday ICC, Paris will take a holistic view of the UCP, the ISBP, the Opinion of the ICC Banking Commission et al and harmonise the rules and the procedures in the best interest of all concerned.

It should be clearly understood that all opinion and observations are solely that of the author, the ICC (Paris) or any other agency having nothing to do with them.

Rupnarayan Bose
rnbose@gmail.com
Calcutta, India
April, 2023

+++

PREFACE TO THE FIRST EDITION

The ICC Uniform Customs and Practice for Documentary Credits (UCP) was first published by the International Chamber of Commerce (ICC) in 1933. Revised versions were issued in 1951, 1962, 1974, 1983 and 1994 respectively. After being in operation for more than twelve years from 1 January 1994, UCP 500 was replaced by UCP 600 on 1 July 2007.

This revision of the UCP, the sixth since its inception, was named by the ICC as the '2007 Revision'. The major changes in the current revised edition, as proclaimed by the ICC, were as follows:

a. a leaner set of rules, with 39 articles rather than 49 articles of UCP 500;

b. a new section of 'definitions', containing terms such as 'honour' and 'negotiation';

c. a replacement of the expression 'reasonable time' with a definite number of days for examining and determining compliance of documents;

d. a new provision concerning addresses of the beneficiary and the applicant;

e. an expanded discussion of 'original documents';

f. re-drafted transport articles aimed at resolving confusion over the identification of carriers and agents.

This list provides a ready answer to the frequently asked question, 'From UCP 500 to UCP 600, what had changed?' To those who have been closely associated over the years with documentary credits in general, and UCP 500 in particular, this list can do little to satisfy their curiosity about the real changes that the latest 'Revision' has brought about. For them to be satisfied with this response would be to miss the wood for the trees. For, from UCP 500 to UCP 600, the changes are several and very significant.

In fact, what the ICC did on this occasion was to move away completely from its earlier practice of making changes line by line. Instead, the emphasis was on making technical changes to the document as a whole. Therefore, the issues were tackled in a more holistic manner. The starting point of this process was by taking into account all the developments since the implementation of UCP 500 in 1994. URR 525[1] and ISP 98[2], for example, were published and implemented much

---

[1] URR, Uniform Rules for Bank-to-bank Reimbursement under Documentary Credits, Publication No. 525, and ISP, International Standby Practices, are ICC publications.

[2] ISP 98 is a set of rules designed to facilitate the domestic and international use of standby letters of credit. ISP 98 addresses several topics that were not addressed at all by UCP 500 or that were addressed only generally by UCP 500. In addition, ISP 98

after UCP 500 came into operation. Other developments that were required to be taken into account included those by way of opinions and decisions expressed by the ICC, disputes referred to it for disposal, and results of court actions. Further, just seven of the articles of UCP 500 had given rise to 58 per cent of all the ICC opinions, views and clarifications. There was an urgent need to examine these 'problem' articles since they were the cause of maximum doubts and debates. The revision process also provided an opportunity to examine and take a view on several other issues – some major ones, and others not exactly so but serious nonetheless – that required attention and a decision from the ICC. The purpose of these changes was to make the UCP more robust, a stand-alone set of rules, with an ability to meet the needs of the future.

The nature of changes introduced made the study of UCP 600 and its comparative analysis against UCP 500 a difficult task. For all 'revisions' up to and including UCP 500, one could place the original articles on one side, the revised ones right next to them, and carry out a very satisfactory comparison of the two versions. With UCP 600 it was hardly, if at all, possible to do so - least of all because the articles in UCP 600 were fewer in number. In reality, all the important topics have been retained, the critical issues suitably dealt with. It is true that some of the

---

contains several rules crafted for standby letters of credit that differ from their UCP 500 counterparts. ISP 98 came into operation from 1 January 1999.

articles from UCP 500 have been dropped; on the other hand, some new ones have also been added. Most have been revised, reworded or redrafted, making point to point comparison a futile exercise. Part I of this book provides a complete picture of the evolution of the UCP and the key issues that shaped UCP 600.

Reverting to the earlier question, from UCP 500 to UCP 600 what indeed *has* changed? If one were to give a brief reply, many things. In reality, the changes go deeper, are fundamental in nature, and could be termed as significant in more sense than one, making UCP 600 a far better document than its immediate predecessor.

While planning to write this book on UCP 600, the main concern was about the best way to bring out these changes, the most effective way to compare the original articles of UCP 500 and their transformation in UCP 600. One obvious way would have been to begin with the articles of UCP 500, identify their counterparts in the new revision, highlight the changes and explain the key issues. This style of comparison has been followed by some, especially while making presentations in seminars and workshops on UCP 600.

This book does not tread that path. The main reason is that living in the era of UCP 600, the present-day user would benefit the most if the focus was on the articles of UCP 600 themselves, on the implications of the currently operational clauses and articles rather than on its predecessor, UCP 500. In this book, therefore, the comparison and analysis begin with UCP 600, its articles being studied for its own merit and import. The analysis of the articles of UCP 600 was complemented by simultaneous comparisons with UCP 500 – essentially to better understand and appreciate the *changes* introduced.

The book begins with the various stages of transition of UCP 500 right up to its present-day version that is UCP 600 today. Part 1 of this book, comprising three chapters, deals with the compulsions for the revision and the initial considerations that influenced the revision process. These chapters outline the process, the issues that came up for consideration, the manner in which these issues were resolved, the reasons for accepting or rejecting certain changes, highlight the changes that were finally made in the UCP and the reasons for the same. The evolution of the UCP 600 is an interesting story that is required to be told, in detail. It provides essential background to the articles that are the very foundations of documentary credit operations today. Without this background information the study of the revised articles would remain imperfect, the understanding of UCP 600 incomplete.

Part 2 of this book takes the reader from the first article of UCP 600 to the last. The articles have been compared and analysed against their counterparts in UCP 500. The changes from their earlier versions have been highlighted and the rationale explained in depth and with great care.

Wherever necessary, additional information has been appended by way of author's notes and comments. The process is sure to make for a far better understanding of the articles of UCP 600, and a greater appreciation of their implications and application.

[Deleted]

The story about the evolution of UCP 600 is reconstructed from available and published sources in the public domain. However, it should be clarified that the statements, comments, observations, interpretations, claims and conclusions contained in this book have not been endorsed by the ICC or any of its officers. They are solely of the author of this book (sometimes coloured by his own imagination), who takes responsibility for the same, as well as for any error or omission that may have taken place in spite of every effort made for presenting an accurate picture on the subject and the reconstruction thereof.

'From UCP 500 to UCP 600, what has changed?' is the question that still remains to be addressed. The response to this question is available in chapter 2. Briefly stated, the most impressive feature of UCP 600 is the improvement in the overall approach to the presentation of the articles. For example, the articles are now arranged in a logical sequence. The topics and subjects are rearranged and grouped together under appropriate titles (which was not the case earlier). Complex, long drawn-out articles have been simplified, their lengths reduced. The language is simple, easy to understand and very user-friendly. Gaps and grey areas in the rules have been removed. Critical articles have been redrafted or reworded, new rules have been framed where necessary to remove ambiguities and re-establish procedures. The newly-introduced articles on definitions and interpretations have helped greatly to contribute to the foregoing. Overall, this version is a far better product than its earlier counter-parts.

Having said that, UCP 600 still appears to have a few shortcomings. One of the major issues that remain unresolved to this day is the proper interpretation of the term 'negotiation'. By including a definition of this term in UCP 600 a delicate attempt has been made to provide a solution to this long-outstanding problem. However, the attempt falls far short of its objectives. The definition itself appears incorrect. It also leaves unanswered several related questions. The issue concerning 'negotiation' has been discussed in detail in chapter 3.

A number of other articles in the new UCP 600 contain clauses that require a review. The views of this author on these articles, the issues and the suggestions for their resolution have been presented in chapter 3[3].

Since 1933, the UCP has provided the foundation and acted as the backbone for documentary credit operations worldwide. Its most recent version, UCP 600, is sure to do

---

[3] This author's book titled "Beyond Trade Finance" (Notion Press, April 2022) also examines selected UCP 600 articles in greater detail.

no less. I hope that this book and the analysis of the articles of UCP 600 are found useful by the bankers, exporters, importers, trainers, the trade associations, those in the trading community who use letters of credit, as well as everyone who deals with documentary credits for one reason or another. If the analysis and commentaries contained in the following pages contribute to a better understanding of the UCP and thereby facilitate international trade, my efforts would have been amply rewarded. All suggestions for improvement of this book are most welcome and would be greatly appreciated.

+++

ACKNOWLEDGEMENT

(First edition)

This book could not have been written without the permission given by the International Chamber of Commerce, Paris, France to reproduce selected sections of the articles that make up UCP 600. I owe my thanks to them for the same and for their continued support.

This book is based on UCP 600. The articles and the background material about the evolution of the UCP are the foundations of this book. Without these, the book would have remained incomplete. The story about the evolution of UCP 600 had to be necessarily gleaned and reconstructed from several published and publicly available sources. These sources include commentaries, news reports, announcements and reviews about the progress and the drafting of the revised UCP that were released from time to time. To their authors I acknowledge my debt and owe my thanks.

My special thanks to Mr. Gary Collyer, Technical Advisor to the ICC Commission on Banking Technique and Practice and the driving force behind the revision, for his very informative and illuminating articles on the revision process. These articles and the workshops on UCP 600 held in 2007 in India have helped me greatly in completing my project even without being in the thick of things.

I acknowledge the contributions of the many chambers of commerce, commercial banks and other institutions for the opportunity given to me to speak on UCP 600. The continued interactions with them and the active interests of the participants of my seminars and workshops have helped me in crystallising my thoughts, honing my presentations and in writing this book.

Finally, I would be failing in my duty if I do not make a mention of the entire team at Macmillan India Limited, my publishers, who stood by me over the years in spite of all my inadequacies as an author. Their active involvement and contribution in giving shape to each of my books and helping me to realise my dreams, are beyond measure.

+++

SECTION 1:

The Origin of the Revisions and Initial Considerations

CHAPTER 1

THE EVOLUTION OF UCP 600

1.1 Background

Most of what follows is now a part of history – a matter for the record books. These are narrated here to bring out the working of the ICC, the issues involved and how these were addressed, the enormity of the task at hand and the process to deal with them. Just like visiting a place without knowing anything about its history is an exercise in futility, it is important to understand the history and the issues under consideration for a better understanding of the UCP.

On 25 October 2006 by a unanimous vote of 91 to nil, the International Chamber of Commerce (ICC) Commission on Banking Technique and Practice (the ICC Banking Commission) approved UCP 600, the ICC's revised rules on documentary credits. UCP 600 came into effect on 1 July 2007. In order to set the stage for further discussions on the subject let us revisit the events leading up to this landmark occasion.[4]

Since the early days of letters of credit, bankers and banking groups have been collecting and documenting banking practices. The national rules established prior to the development of the first Uniform Customs and Practice for Documentary Credits ('UCP') were, in fact, collections of banking practice in a number of individual countries. These national documents, created in the early 1900s, established basic rules for letters of credit in Argentina, Czechoslovakia, France, Germany, Italy, Sweden and the United States. The first paragraph of the Regulations Affecting Export Commercial Letters of Credit created in the United States in 1920 stated: 'Payments under Export Commercial Credits advised to the undersigned are made in conformity with the following regulations, which are in accord with the standard practice adopted by the New York Bankers Commercial Credit Conference of 1920'. These rules and practices, distributed by banks to their correspondents throughout the world, were simply an articulation of how banks handled letters of credit and were intended to inform their

---

[4] Source: Dan Taylor, President and CEO of the International Financial Services Association and Vice Chairman of the ICC Commission on Banking Technique and Practice; Appendix to ISBP, ICC Publication No. 681.

correspondents of the practices they followed in their own countries. Ultimately, these practices were documented more formally and on a global scale in the first UCP. At that time it was called Uniform Customs and Practice for Commercial Documentary Credits. UCP 600 is the sixth revision of the UCP since its first publication in 1933.

The revision of UCP 500 began in May 2003 when the Banking Commission put its seal of approval to a resolution to launch the exercise for review of UCP 500 and to draft a new set of rules. As had happened earlier for the revision of UCP 400, the process that was set in motion in 2003 was to take a little over three years and many man-hours to complete.

The revision process was begun with the constitution of what was called as the 'Drafting Group'. It was constituted with nine members. These nine members provided effective representation for Eastern and Western Europe, Asia and North America. Room was created within the Drafting Group for a representative from SWIFT (Society for Worldwide Interbank Financial Telecommunication). This was to ensure that the implications of strategic changes to the rules could be assessed right at their inception, and to evaluate if any change was required to be made to the MT 7XX series of messages generated by SWIFT. (The MT7XX series deals with documentary credit related messages.)

A new concept to manage the revision process was simultaneously implemented. In accordance with suggestions made, the Drafting Group was supplemented by what was called the 'Consulting Group', to work in tandem with the Drafting Group. The Consulting Group included not only representatives from the banking profession, but also from other professional bodies like that of transport operators, lawyers, insurers – groups who also had a stake in the UCP revision.

The Consulting Group, initially formed with 37 members from 26 countries, was later expanded to comprise 41 members. The members of the Consulting Group were to comment on and, if necessary, suggest amendments to drafts of the revision released from time to time by the Drafting Group. Through this process the Drafting Group wanted to ensure that the drafts were subjected to a thorough review before being despatched to the National Committees globally for their comments, thereby saving considerable time.

The Consulting Group was charged with several specific responsibilities. These included the examination of new concepts and ideas thrown up during the review process -- to confirm that they were, as far as possible, in line with a country's local and legal requirements. Another objective was to ensure that the language and terminologies used in the final draft could be comfortably translated into native languages of countries that were subscribers to and users of the UCP (more about this, later). Last, but not the least, one of the major ideas behind the formation of the Consulting Group was to sort out, discuss and debate, and thus hopefully reduce the number of comments and consultation papers from the large number of member countries that would have to be examined[5] before a draft could actually be evolved for formal submission to the National Committees worldwide.

1.2 Schedule of events

The first ever presentation was made during the New Delhi conference in December 2003 to the ICC Banking Commission, where it was decided that the first draft of the revised UCP would be despatched by the drafting group around the first quarter of 2004, well before the next Banking Commission meeting scheduled for 10-11 May 2004. The time gap was provided to enable the National Committees of member countries to receive and respond to the first draft comments. In this meeting of the drafting group, comments of the various National Committees were to be reviewed and discussed.

The road map was as follows. The May 2004 meeting was to be followed by a meeting of the Drafting Group in September 2004 in the US. The revised drafts were then to be sent, once again, to ICC National Committees for their comment. The comments received from the National Committees were to be discussed by the Consulting Group and the Drafting Group. This was to be followed by

---

[5] Reportedly, the group drafting UCP 500 had to read through some 5,000 sets of comments before the group came up with a final text.

the presentation of new drafts to the Banking Commission at its meeting in Moscow in October 2004. The Drafting Group was then to meet for three days for review and re-examination of the comments and suggestions made by the participants in the meeting at Moscow. The conclusions arrived at after the three-day meeting of the Drafting Group were then to be incorporated into a fresh draft of the UCP.

In order to ensure continuation of the revision process, provision was made for a third Banking Commission meeting during 2005, with one or more of the meetings marked exclusively for the UCP.

An outline of the initial cycle of discussions, review, revision, comments and observations, further review etc. was furnished to illustrate the revision process that the UCP 500 was subjected to. The process, as could very well be judged, involved the stake holders (all sections that had an interest in the functionality of the UCP), the member countries and their respective National Committees, representatives that ensured geographical representation, and the experts themselves. It was a massive exercise, by any standard.

1.3 Why was this revision necessary

UCP 500 had been working (arguably) well for more than 10 years when the ICC decided to initiate the process of revising this document. The trade and the industry had become accustomed to its provisions, had begun to understand and grasp the nuances of its various articles, and had come to accept the clauses – warts and all. In order to improve the operations of the UCP the ICC, through its Banking Commission, had also issued a series of 'Position Papers', opinions and clarifications to resolve disputes, dispel confusions, and correct some of the negative practices that had taken root in the period during which the UCP had been in operation.

The ICC had taken additional initiatives to explain how the practices articulated in the UCP were to be applied by the users of documentary credits. The aim was to reduce discrepancies in documents, reduce rejections and delays, and thus improve the international trade environment. To achieve its objectives, the ICC brought out a detailed guideline called The International Standard Banking Practices (ISBP), ICC Publication No. 645[6]. The two-year long process began with its May 2000 meeting when it established a Task Force to document international standard banking practices for the examination of documents presented under documentary credits issued under UCP 500. Consisting of 200

---

[6] This document was replaced by ISBP, ICC Publication No. 681 with effect from 1 July 2007. However, since ISBP, ICC Publication No. 645 was in operation throughout the period covered by the revision process (the latter version coming into being much later), all reference to the ISBP in this book are to Publication No. 645, unless specifically stated otherwise. (ISBP 745 is currently in operation.)

individual articles and articles, this document[7] was formally approved by the ICC Banking Commission at its meeting in Rome, Italy on 30 October 2002.

The ISBP incorporated all comments and suggestions received and discussed, and all relevant amendments to the document offered by the National Committees of its member countries. The objective was to make the statements in the ISBP as 'international' as possible. The Task Force had also been careful to ensure that this document was consistent with the provisions of the UCP and with opinions, decisions, and Position Papers of the Banking Commission, as well as applicable DOCDEX[8] decisions. The ISBP thus reflected international standard banking practice for the benefit of all parties to a documentary credit and supplemented the provisions of UCP 500. It should be noted that ISBP 645 was released only six months prior to the decision to take up the revision of UCP 500.

---

[7] International Standard Banking Practice for the Examination of Documents under Documentary Credits (ISBP), ICC document 470/951 rev 4.

[8] DOCDEX is a speedy and reliable dispute settlement mechanism providing for a document-based expert decision made by three experts, scrutinized by the technical adviser of the ICC Banking Commission and issued by the International Centre for Expertise. The DOCDEX decision is not binding unless the parties have agreed otherwise. In most instances, the parties can expect the final opinion six to twelve weeks after the ICC has received the request, but exceptionally complex cases could take longer.

Another noteworthy point is the fact that several key members of the Task Force that shaped the ISBP were those who were later mobilised by the ICC to revise UCP 500. One would have assumed that, with the publication of the ISBP (along with the Position Papers and other releases referred earlier), the shortcomings (if any) of the UCP had been taken care of, at least for some time to come.

Apparently, that was not to be. One could not, therefore, be faulted if one wondered why, after such great efforts to address current issues facing the UCP, would a new UCP be at all necessary. Any apprehension that all the hard work of the past was going to be undone if, once again, the UCP 500 was revised, could not be entirely discounted either.

The ripple effect of the revision of a critical document like the UCP could affect many. For, a new UCP would inevitably translate into fresh rounds of comments and criticisms, debates and discussions, a process of unlearning and relearning, retraining and re-educating personnel. The corporate sector, those in the world of business, insurers, transporters, and the other users of letters of credit would also have to go through the same process. Some of the critical documents, like the ISBP and the standard forms in use across the industry may have to be modified too to fall in line with the new order. Any change in the UCP could thus affect a wide spectrum of users across several industries around the world.

Under these circumstances, there had to be very compelling reasons for undertaking the revision process. Were there reasons enough, or compulsions so overriding, to revise the UCP?

1.4 The compulsions for revising the UCP

There is no reason to believe that the ICC was not aware of the situation as it existed at the time it decided to go for an all-new UCP. As stated earlier, the process was going to be cumbersome and time consuming, involving a large section of interested parties across several industries. Perhaps aware of this backdrop, the ICC begun the revision process with formation of the 'Task Force' and a clear view of what it wanted to achieve through the revision process.

The Task Force, with the aim to put form and substance to the new UCP 600, put forward its recommendations regarding the approach it had in mind to the revision process. The main recommendation of the Task Force was the suggestion to have a holistic approach to the revision. Their suggestion was to move away from the practice followed till then to make changes line by line. Instead, the suggested way forward was to go for technical changes if, in their judgement, the situation so warranted.

Further, the Task Force suggested that the revision should take into account the developments since the launch of UCP 500 in 1994 (referred briefly in the preface to this book). This recommendation came in the light of major developments such as the release of the Uniform Rules for Bank-to-Bank Reimbursement (ICC Publication No. 525), URR 525 (published in November 1995, coming into effect from 1 July 1996), the International Standby Practices (ISP 98) on 1 January 1999, the International Standard Banking Practices (ISBP), ICC Publication No. 645 on 30 October 2002, and the eUCP in 2003.

There were other developments that had also to be considered. Among them were the DOCDEX cases and situations arising as a result of court actions, along with Opinions and decisions expressed by the ICC in response to various issues, arguments, disputes that were brought to its attention for clarification. *It had been found that just seven*[9] *of the articles of UCP 500 had given rise to 58% of all the ICC opinions, views and clarifications.* The revision process had to be an inclusive one, taking into account the contentious articles, factoring in the ICC opinions and decisions as also the post-UCP 500 developments.

The aim was to take a fresh look at all the developments since UCP 500 was first issued, evaluate them against the present day requirements, address such other issues as may be necessary to identify and resolve, and in the process come up with a version of the UCP that would not be dependent on the multitude of 'opinions', Position Papers, definitions, clarifications, cross-references and

---

[9] Refer to chapter 2, section 2.2.1.

the like for accurate interpretation. The conviction, therefore, was that the revised version would surely benefit from, and incorporate (with modifications wherever necessary), the developments since the release of the original UCP 500 affecting its interpretation. Thus, the final revised version should be a product capable of standing on its own strength.

1.5 The initial considerations

The major objective, as was evident, was to bring out a 'cleaner', modern version of the UCP. The exercise also provided an opportunity to come up with an *improved* version of the UCP. It was essential that the letter of credit be perceived as a payment vehicle rather than a means of avoiding payment. To the extent that better drafting of the UCP could contribute to that end, this was one of the primary objectives of any revision [10], an objective that deserved plaudits.

As with any revision, the proposed exercise simultaneously provided the Drafting Group with the opportunity to take a critical look at all the articles to weigh their relevance and utility in the context of the present day. The revision also provided motivation to consider new concepts, procedures and practices that were already in existence, or were necessary, to make the UCP robust and acceptable for time to come.

---

[10] DC Insight, ICC Publication, July-September 2004.

The revision process also provided the Task Force a window of opportunity to examine other contentious issues that had not been resolved till then. The major one among them was that of tackling the term 'negotiation'[11]. Some, including eminent experts on documentary credits and a few members of the Drafting Group, clearly stated that even they did not understand the exact meaning of the term 'negotiation'[12]. Others wanted the word to be completely removed from the UCP. It was necessary to put the matter to rest, some day.

Another issue that called for attention was that of language. The December 2003 meeting of the Banking Commission held in New Delhi noted that 'the English wording of the UCP did not always translate well into other languages'. By way of an example, the meeting was informed that the word 'draft' had no Italian equivalent. Owing to widespread use of the UCP, including in countries other than those who used English as a primary means of communication, care had to be taken to use words that could be translated without distortion in meaning.

Some of the other issues that had to be addressed included Standby LCs, eUCP, and deferred payment

---

[11] See articles titled (i) Some random thoughts on the UCP, (ii) Negotiation: the concept, (iii) Re-defining 'negotiation', (iv) What is 'negotiation', and why it must stay in the UCP in the book Beyond Trade Finance by this author.

[12] Ibid.

credit (DPC). Implemented from 1 January 1999, ISP 98 (ICC Publication No. 590) was the product of more than five years of drafting. ISP 98 had been created specifically to address generally accepted practice, custom, and usage relating to standby letters of credit (SBLC). Since ISP 98 took care of issues relating exclusively to standby LCs, it had to be decided whether there was a continued need for the UCP too to be made applicable to standby LCs [13] (refer to article 1 of UCP 500).

Next, about deferred payment credits (DPC). Logically speaking, when two parties expressly agree to abide by certain provisions, rules or terms of an agreement, these same terms should be examined carefully to see if they have a bearing on the transactions themselves, and in the resolution of disputes. If a transaction is subject to the terms of the UCP, courts are inclined to take into account its applicable provisions while deciding cases relating to international trade. 'ICC Decisions, while they do not carry legal force or overturn court decisions, are widely read by the courts as an indication of how UCP 500 should be interpreted.'[14]

---

[13] In actual fact, what happened was that the articles of ISP 98 acted as a resource for the new articles of UCP 600. Several of those from ISP 98 were transposed (with modifications, wherever necessary) and incorporated in the revised draft of UCP 600.

[14] *'ICC clarifies 'original document' language in UCP 500'*, ICC Comments on 'Original Documents'; Paris, 12 July 1999.

Unfortunately, UCP 500 made no mention of deferred payment credits (DPC). Although deferred payment credits were in common use in trade and commerce, the UCP did not appear to recognise this financial instrument. UCP 500 was applicable only to negotiation, acceptance, and payment credits. The users of DPCs, therefore, found no recourse in or support from the UCP when disputes relating to DPCs came up in the courts. Since the UCP did not specifically cover DPCs, the courts in their turn found no reason to extend the provision of the UCP to resolve disputes regarding DPCs. Over the years, the by now famous Banco Santander[15] case and other court decisions had added to the confusion, leaving all concerned without a clear direction. There was, thus, an urgent need address this issue[16] in the subsequent revisions of the UCP.

Finally, there was this small matter about eUCP. It had been approved and implemented by the ICC in 2003. A new version of the UCP was bound to affect the operation

---

[15] Banco Santander discounted a deferred payment letter of credit it had confirmed. Fraud was discovered between presentation and maturity. The issuing bank successfully argued that, because fraud was detected before maturity and the confirming bank had no authority to discount, the issuing bank did not have to reimburse Banco Santander.

[16] A few members of the Commission did not want the provisions on deferred payment credit included in UCP 600 because they felt this unfairly pushed a greater fraud risk on to the issuing bank, and therefore on the applicant. Others felt they should be included because it should not be the confirming bank that should bear this risk.

of eUCP in some area or the other. The issue was whether to *merge* its provisions with the revised UCP or revise and amend it in line with the revision being made in UCP 500 while continuing with it as a *separate* document. A decision on this had to be taken.

So there were questions, questions, and more questions that cried out for a solution.

1.6 UCP revision: The early phase

The Task Force and the Drafting Group, thus, began their revision exercise keeping issues such as the foregoing and a few others in focus. The first draft was planned to be circulated somewhere during the first quarter of 2004. After allowing for a few weeks to receive responses from the National Committees of various countries, their comments were set to be discussed and debated at the Banking Commission's meeting scheduled for 10-11 May 2004 in Paris.

The ICC Banking Commission met in Paris in May 2004, devoting one full day in discussing the draft of the articles 1 to 19 of UCP 500 revised and submitted by the UCP Drafting Group. Some weeks later, the Consulting Group received for review drafts of the next ten articles (revised versions of the articles 20 to 29 of UCP 500). It should, however, be noted that the revised drafts of articles 20 to 29 did not include those articles in the UCP relating to transport.

Issues that were taken up for discussion at the Paris meeting included the following[17]:

a. Should 'applicant' be defined in the text of the rules?

b. Should all credits be considered to be irrevocable?

c. What should be done about letters of credit issued by non-banks?

d. Should the question of drafts on applicants be addressed?

e. How was one to treat drafts in general in the new rules?[18]

f. What should be done with regard to the term 'negotiation'?

---

[17] *DC Insight*, ICC Publication, July-September 2004.

[18] Di Ninni, a member of the Consulting Group, was reported to have said that there was no equivalent for the word 'draft' in the Italian language. Italian banks, in order to get around the problem, had special implicit agreements with other banks and other clients. (First presentation to the Banking Commission, *DCInsight*, issue of Jan-March 2004). This apart, the issue continues to plague the ICC, which came out with two documents viz., (1) Guidance Paper - the use of drafts (bills of exchange) under documentary credits – Executive summary, and (2) Additional material relating to the Guidance Paper - the use of drafts under documentary credits prepared by the Executive Committee of the ICC Banking Commission - both dated 08 Jan 2019.

g. What about the situation where a credit was subject to a sight payment by a nominated bank that did not pay?

h. Should 'signing' and 'confirmation' be defined?

i. Should the words 'without delay' be defined in more detail?

j. Should there be time limits for amendments?

k. What is the effect of a non-operative letter of credit and how does it work?

l. How should the rules attempt to clarify some of the problems raised by controversial court decisions, such as the *Banco Santander* case?

All these issues provide a very interesting background to the development of UCP 600 as it stands today. They also provide a rare insight into the evolution of the UCP and the articles as we see them today. For practitioners of the UCP, it is necessary to understand the issues listed earlier, the reasons why they were considered as 'issues' requiring a decision, understand the approach of the Drafting Group in addressing these issues, and finally the manner for their resolution. Some of the issues would, therefore, be taken up separately in due course for a fuller discussion.

It may be mentioned in passing that the background to item no. xii above is furnished later in this chapter under section 1.8.8. Negotiation[19] (item no. vi) is an issue that has proved to be vexing to the extreme. The term continued to fox many an expert over the years, has done so for more than 80 years since the inception of the UCP, and still eludes a satisfactory and universally acceptable definition. The matter of *defining* certain terms (item no. viii) such as applicant, signing, confirmation and negotiation arose because in the new UCP a section to define certain standard and oft-repeated terms was under consideration.[20]

Following the meeting of the Banking Commission, the Drafting Group met for three days, working on improving the structure of the first nineteen articles that had been received as the first lot. The Drafting Group simultaneously worked on developing the other articles that had not been commented on till then[21].

1.7 Continuation of the revision process

By the end of the year 2004 all the articles of UCP 500 (except article 48) had been redrafted at least once. During the course of 2004 all the revised versions (in some cases, second and third drafts) had been sent to National Committees of member countries around the

---

[19] Refer to footnote number 10.

[20] Later, the proposals took final shape in UCP 600 as articles 2 and 3 titled 'Definitions' and 'Interpretations' respectively.

[21] The Consulting Group responded on 18 June 2004 with its comments on the entire revised draft.

world and other ICC commissions for their views and response. The progress made by the working groups had given rise to the possibility that if all went well the final version could, perhaps, be in place by the end of 2005 and that the final product, UCP 600, could come into effect sometimes in 2006[22].

Almost two years had passed since the ICC Banking Commission took up the task of revising the UCP. However, a study of the comments received from various National Committees showed that there were several issues, including some of those identified as 'key issues', for which no real consensus had emerged till then among the members. The result was that the Drafting Group was not sure as to the position that it could take in finalising the articles of the revised UCP. The ICC, therefore, decided to hold a special meeting of the Banking Commission to discuss the draft of the proposed document. It was felt that an open and free discussion on these diverse positions could help the members as well as the Drafting Group reach a conclusion. Therefore, a full meeting of the ICC Banking Commission was held in Dublin on 27 and 28 June, 2005.

At this meeting (later referred to as the 'Dublin Meet') more than 170 bankers, lawyers, consultants and

---

[22] As we know now, the expectation was premature. This did not come to pass. The final version was approved by the Banking Commission in Paris on 25 October 2006, for implementation from 1 July 2007.

transport specialists were in attendance. They had before them for discussion the fourth revised draft of the new UCP articles 1 to 19, the second revised draft of article 30 (roughly equivalent to article 23 of UCP 500), and the second draft of new articles 39 to 46 (partial drawings/shipments, instalment drawings/shipments, extension of expiry date, etc.). During more than eight hours of intensive debate, the UCP Drafting Group presented and explained the latest wording of the revised rules based on the ICC National Committee comments and Drafting Group input.[23] Those who attended the meeting got a first-hand feel of the issues under discussion, the thinking process of the Drafting Group and the Banking Commission on these issues. They also had an opportunity to express their opinion and contribute towards the evolution of the new UCP. At the end of the meeting, the participants had a better understanding of the status of the revision, as well as a complete overview of the issues under discussion.

1.8 The key issues

In order to appreciate UCP 600, and the transformation it has undergone from its previous incarnation called UCP 500, it is essential for us to discuss in detail the issues that the ICC National Committees, the Drafting Group,

---

[23] The new articles 20 to 29 were not discussed in depth at that time, since the Drafting Group had yet to incorporate National Committee comments on them.

and the Banking Commission spent considerable time in reviewing. The 'key issues', as the identified issues were called, were the ones listed as under:

1. Capitalising defined terms and words
2. And/or
3. On its face
4. 'Parties' or 'banks'
5. Reasonable time
6. International Standard Banking Practices (ISBP)
7. Negotiation
8. Discounting of Deferred Payments
9. Article 28 of UCP 500
10. Article 30 of UCP 500

In the pages that follow we take up each of these key issues, examine the reasons for their being identified as such, and understand how these issues were resolved or finally disposed of. The process would help us to understand their relevance in the context of the final version of UCP 600. Documentary credit aficionados will surely find the deliberations of quite some interest (at some places, of amusement, too).

1.8.1 Capitalising defined terms and words

We begin with issues that were influenced by language and interpretation[24]. A reading of UCP 500 and its earlier versions would show that the first letter of several words including common nouns were being capitalised (began with a capital letter). The words 'advising bank', 'issuing bank', 'negotiation', 'payment', 'draft', 'credit' etc., though not proper nouns, had their first letters in capital. In addition, article 2 of the draft version of UCP 600 was conceived to define certain terms used in the articles that were to follow. The issue was whether the terms that were to be defined and included in this article (titled 'Definitions') be capitalised or not.

In the Dublin Meet, it was reported that National Committees of eighteen countries (out of thirty-seven) voted for capitalisation. Fifteen were against capitalisation. Four countries opted out or offered other solutions, including two voting for defined terms to be in bold text[25]. The Drafting Group created a draft with capitalisation but found the look and style not to be acceptable (in some cases every other word being capitalised). The result was very confusing indeed.

---

[24] The appeal from several sections was also for the use of 'more plain language' in the UCP.

[25] It just goes to show how even an apparently simple issue – that of capitalisation, for example – can divide the house.

As a final outcome, to the relief of one and all, and in line with current drafting techniques for rules and agreements, in UCP 600 capitalisation was done away with.

1.8.2 And/or

In response to the feedback received, the Drafting Group did make a conscious attempt to avoid the use of 'and/or' in the new rules. In the Paris meeting held on 24-25 October 2005, a couple of countries wanted 'and/or' to be retained. The issue was considered, but finally, in contrast to UCP 500, its use in UCP 600 has been kept to the barest minimum.

1.8.3 On its Face

This is a typical instance of language and interpretation causing untold confusion. Used in the context of examination of documents in UCP 500 the phrase, translated literally, could be taken to mean the *front* of the document as opposed to the *back*. Some felt that the words meant different things in different languages. National Committees of some countries expressed an apprehension that on translation, the expression failed to communicate the precise meaning as had been intended in the UCP. The feeling in certain quarters, therefore, was that the expression could continue to be a possible source of confusion if its present form was retained in the subsequent drafts of the UCP.

Yet a few others disagreed with these views. They felt that there wasn't sufficient reason to delete the expression 'on its face' from the UCP. According to them, the phrase had been around for a very long time. It was well-entrenched in practices and procedures of LC practitioners around the world. They were firm in their belief that those who were familiar with the phrase *did* know its purpose and its meaning. The expression 'on its face', contrary to its literal interpretation, in effect referred to 'the review of a document in line with international standard banking practice and the features of the document itself'. The users of the UCP and letters of credit surely knew that a document was read for its data content – which was what the expression 'on its face' sought to convey. The expression, therefore, served a useful purpose. According to a group of participants, removal of the expression could lead to misunderstanding and confusion.

The Drafting Group reflected a similar sentiment. It felt 'that such reference is warranted in this place so as to maintain the position that is recognised by the courts of what information, page etc. the document checker is expected to review.' The courts had used the phrase and it had a certain value to the legal profession. The courts had looked at the expression 'on its face' not to mean the front or the back or the side of any document, but to mean that *one should not go beyond the documents*. The concern was that if the phrase was completely removed from the rules, it would upset the process. Its removal might create confusion in the minds of the judiciary because judges might wonder why it was taken out. If the phrase was retained in the text the reason for the same would have to be explained, and if they were left out that would also have to be explained too. Because, if the words were taken out without an explanation, it could create more confusion than allowing them to stay and saying nothing (it had been there, anyway!). To remove it completely would require its replacement by a similar phrase to explain that no change in philosophy has been made. It was a typical Catch-22 situation.

At the Commission meeting in Dublin, the National Committees had been asked by the Drafting Group to provide responses to a number of the key issues still remaining to be decided. On this particular issue 25 countries voted to remove the reference to 'on its face' and 12 disagreed. However, the Drafting Group believed there was a case for retaining 'on its face' in (at least) one location within the rules, if for no other reason than simply to reinforce the position and understanding of the term as it continued to exist for reasons outlined in the preceding paragraphs in this section.

In the end, except at one place in the final version of UCP 600, the expression 'on its face' was removed from all places where it appeared in UCP 500, especially the articles on transport. The UCP 600 makes reference to 'on their face' only in article 14(a) of UCP 600 under 'Standard for Examination of Documents'.

1.8.4 'Parties' or 'Banks'

In drafting UCP 600, the Drafting Group was mindful of the growing practice of LCs issued by corporate entities. The prevalent thinking was that the word 'banks' should be retained, notwithstanding the recognition by the ICC that non-banks *could* also issue LCs - as was commonplace for the larger US companies when dealing with suppliers in Asia. At one point it was suggested that the word 'bank' be retained in the UCP, but its definition be expanded to include non-banks (parties other than banks) as issuers of documentary credits. The bottom-line was whether UCP 600 should recognise that practice (of non-banks issuing LCs) and the terminologies be consequently amended everywhere in the UCP – from, for example, 'issuing bank' to 'issuer' (with a definition – by including a wider definition of 'bank', viz., 'issuer' being the 'party' that issues the credit), 'confirming bank' to 'confirmer' etc., so that the terms referred not only to banks but expanded to include non-banks.

National Committees were requested to indicate their preference for use of either 'party' or 'bank'. The majority of comments from the audience in the Dublin meeting of June 2005 indicated a strong preference for usage of the word 'banks' instead of 'parties'[26]. Out of 37 countries, 27 voted for retention of 'banks' instead of 'parties'.

---

[26] Some of those Commission members who opposed recognition of non-bank issuers said to have felt so strongly on

The ICC's position[27] is that importers are free to issue documentary credits. They are also free to subject these credits to the UCP. No law could prevent that. However, UCP 600 continues to remain 'by the banks, of the banks, for the banks'. Under article 2, a 'credit' has been defined as '...any arrangement, however named or described, that is irrevocable and thereby constitutes a definite undertaking of the issuing *bank* (emphasis added) to honour a complying presentation.' Further, UCP 600 does not refer to an 'issuer' of a credit. Article 2 defines only an 'issuing *bank*' (emphasis added). Credits issued by the non-banks, therefore, continue to remain outside the purview of the UCP.

1.8.5 Reasonable Time

The words 'reasonable time' and 'without delay', as they appear in the UCP, are expressions that do not indicate any cut-and-dried, definitive period. 'Reasonable time' could perhaps fall somewhere between the two expressions 'as fast as possible' and 'without delay' – a period of time that could perhaps be considered adequate for a particular purpose but not (unreasonably) too long. The reason for retention of the expression 'reasonable

---

this point that they threatened to veto the entire draft if any recognition of non-banks was included in the UCP.

[27] Refer to the official opinion, 'When a non-bank issues a letter of credit' dated 30 October 2002 issued by the Department of Policy and Business Practices, the ICC Commission on Banking Technique and Practice.

time' in the UCP all these days was that not all situations could be conceived in advance, defined or put in a strait-jacket. Banks were expected to act in accordance with the intent with which the words had been used, i.e., as expeditiously as possible under a given circumstances. Instead of 'a reasonable time' if the UCP stated, for example, '5 banking days', what would be the penalty for a bank which exceeded those five days? Logically, a breach should attract a penalty. Could such penalty be enforced in practice?[28]

The main ground for the expression to be removed from the rules was its indeterminate nature. It was debatable how many days constituted a 'reasonable time'. The expression could not be expected to be interpreted uniformly all over the world. It did not convey the same meaning to everyone everywhere. Hence, it could not be part of any internationally applicable *rule*. It was reported[29] that the LC community in China was finding the word 'reasonable' to be dangerous. If considered from a legal point of view, a set number of days was preferred. Even otherwise, most people preferred clear definitions and guidelines over indefinite phrases, black-and-white solutions instead of being called to use their best judgement. A definite period was easier to handle.

---

[28] The Drafting Group decided it would not further define 'without delay' as it was not clear what the penalty would be if the party did not act *without delay*.

[29] ICC Asia Annual Survey Conference Series, 2005.

Compliance or its breach was easier to determine. Only if a period was defined, could penalty be imposed for failure to comply with the deadline.

The demand for a fixed number of days had its opponents. Because the complexity of credits varied, the burden of handling one LC requiring a large number of documents differed greatly from an LC requiring just a couple of documents. The contention was that if the concept of 'reasonable time' was removed, would a bank take any initiative to examine the documents presented and pay well before the maximum period allowed under a credit? If a bank did pay earlier (say, immediately on receipt of documents complying with the terms of the credit), the applicant could well ask why the bank did not extend a credit period to the applicant; why the issuing bank could not wait till the maximum permissible period to debit the applicant's account? On the other hand, in some instances there may be no justification for taking as long as five or seven days to examine the documents and remit to or reimburse the beneficiary. The expression 'reasonable time' in the UCP, in all probability, saved the banker from having to justify to either party why the applicant had to part with funds earlier than the maximum period allowed, or why it took more than a day to honour the documents presented under a credit.

The expression 'shall each have a reasonable time, not to exceed seven banking days' thus allowed an elbowroom with a built-in safeguard by way of a cap regarding the outer limit for examination of documents. From the revised expression 'shall each *have a maximum of five banking days*' (emphasis added) it now appears that the ICC was not *reducing* the time from seven to five banking days. Instead the available time was only being *increased* from a shorter time frame (guided by circumstances of each case and practical considerations) to five days under the new UCP. This could lead to a situation where a bank may check the document on day one but delay further action in the mistaken belief that it had until the cut-off time before it took further action. It was also to be considered whether a rigidly defined period could be of disadvantage to the beneficiary and harm the LC instrument by slowing down the credit process.

Even so, the majority of the members desired clarity. When the issue came up for voting at the Dublin Meet of June 2005, all except one country voted for the removal of the all reference to the words 'reasonable time'. It was a clear decision, making life easier for the Drafting Group.[30] The majority vote for deletion came with only a small rider. Fifteen countries wanted the seven-day period in UCP 500 reduced to five days, nine countries preferred

---

[30] In a signed article appearing in *DC Insight*, (late) Ole Malmqvist said, 'For the Drafting Group, that was a nice clear decision, but I wonder if that change will lead to a general delay in payments to beneficiaries. If it does, we trade finance bankers will regret that we deleted it, and in a few years - fewer than if we retain the 'reasonable time' concept - we will have plenty of time to wonder why we did it.' This author is inclined to agree with this view.

six days, ten opted for seven days, and two had no comments to offer as to what the replacement should be. Accepting a suggestion to have a fixed number of days in general, but at the same time give parties the option to set their own time in special circumstances, the new article in UCP 600 has been framed accordingly.

1.8.6 International Standard Banking Practices (ISBP)

The International Standard Banking Practices (ISBP), ICC Publication No. 645[31] was approved by the ICC Banking Commission on 30 October 2002 in Paris. Being of a very recent origin, the contents of the ISBP was relevant to the UCP, in some instances filling up (mainly procedural) gaps left by the UCP itself. (The fact that in the process it also framed some new rules, was not noticed.) During the process of revision, the Drafting Group picked up some of the concepts used in the ISBP and incorporated them into the revised draft of the UCP. (Which again necessitated the revision of ISBP 681 to ISBP 745.)

At the Dublin Meet (27-28 June 2005) some members wanted to incorporate part or all of the ISBP either in the rules or in the commentary that was to follow the publication of UCP 600. But others, and perhaps the

---

[31] Its next revised version, ICC Publication No. 681, containing 185 articles in all, came into effect from 1 July 2007. It was later replaced by ISBP 745.

majority of members, wanted to retain the ISBP as a separate publication. Their opinion was that many standards and concepts found in the ISBP should be retained in that document itself so as not to make the UCP a *manual* (of operation and procedure[32]) as opposed to what it should always remain, i.e., a set of *rules*. A large majority of countries, therefore, voted to retain the ISBP as a separate document.

An equally important question that the members had to address and resolve was how the ISBP should be mentioned (referred to) in the new UCP. The issues related to what was to be the relationship between the ISBP and the UCP, or how it should be reflected in UCP 600. The reference in the UCP could be by way of direct reference to the publication number or a reference to the publication number and ICC opinions, or by making no reference at all.

An overwhelming majority preferred to establish the relationship with the ISBP through the introduction or foreword to UCP 600. A reference to the publication number of the ISBP was not feasible since the document could very well undergo revisions in future, giving rise to new publication number(s)[33]. It was finally agreed that

---

[32] ISBP 745 exceeded its brief and prescribed a number of rules which rightfully should have been in the UCP. It is hoped that with the next revision of the UCP, the ISBP will also be revised so that the domains of the two do not overlap.

[33] Articles of the ISBP that had been moved to UCP 600 were required to be deleted from the ISBP. A few of these articles had

UCP 600 and ISBP 645 would remain as independent and non-overlapping documents.

ISBP Timeline:

a. Standard Banking Practices for the Examination of Documents (SBPED) - standard banking practices: US Council on International Banking / Mexican Bankers Association - issued in 1997

b. ISBP 645 published in 2003

c. ISBP 681 released 2007, to bring it in line with UCP 600: much of the ISBP text remained unchanged although certain alterations had to be made.

d. ISBP 745 - Approval on 17th April 2013. Note that there was no release or implementation date. If a publication, such as ISBP 745, explains how to apply the rules in UCP 600 and the practices that prevail thereunder, it does not have an implementation date that is post the date of approval.

---

also been redrafted to reflect a position *opposite* in meaning to what was there originally in the ISBP. The ICC, therefore, decided to come out with an updated version of the ISBP (not a revision) by the time UCP 600 was to be implemented. (ISBP, Publication No. 681 has since been implemented with effect from 1 July 2007.) Later, after gaining experience of how the new UCP has been working; the ICC is likely to revisit the issue.

1.8.7 Negotiation

This term had defied definition ever since it was first coined in 1933. Why it has defied definition remains an enduring mystery. Over the years attempts have been made to pin down the term and arrive at a definition that all concerned could agree on. Yet, the issue remained as elusive as ever. Strangely, the term 'negotiation' meant different things to different people. This was one of the reasons why it was so difficult to define.

> 'Every LC expert knows exactly what negotiation is/means. But ask any three of them for their interpretation and be prepared to receive three different answers! (Yet another reason to get rid of the term 'negotiation'!)... No one has been able to come up with a definition that everyone can agree on, and our attempt to draft a definition in article 2 of the revised UCP does not help foster a common understanding of what negotiation is.'

These comments about the continuing problems with the term 'negotiation' came from (late) Ole Malmqvist[34], himself a member of the Drafting Group.

Negotiation, clearly, was one of the tougher nuts to crack. There was a strong support for taking it out of the UCP

---

[34] The Late Ole Malmqvist was also a member of the Task Force which wrote the Rules for Bank-to-Bank Reimbursements (URR 525), and was co-Chair of the Task Force on International Standard Banking Practice for the Examination of Documents under Documentary Credits (ISBP), ICC Publication No. 645.

altogether. But there is also an appreciation of the fact that, while the usage of LCs was declining in the US, in some countries, particularly in the Asian Region, negotiation credits were the rule rather than the exception. Therefore, the term had to be retained. But, if it had to be retained it had also to be defined. Therein lay the problem.

During the revision of the UCP the issue inevitably re-surfaced as one of the 'key issues': 'What should be done with regard to the term 'negotiation'?' The endeavour was to include a definition of this term under article 2 of the new revision. The first draft to define 'negotiation', presented to the ICC Commission on Banking Technique and Practice at its meeting on 24 and 25 October 2005 in Paris, France read as follows:

> 'Negotiation means the purchase by the nominated bank of drafts (drawn on a bank other than the nominated bank) and/or documents, by either advancing or agreeing to advance funds to the beneficiary'.

The definition proved unsatisfactory. It was modified after June 2006 to read as the one that was finally incorporated under article 2 in UCP 600.[35]

---

[35] The definition did not help to resolve the confusion. Read more about it in the articles (see footnote 10) in the book *Beyond trade finance,* by this author

1.8.8 Discounting of deferred payment

The controversial *Banco Santander* court case underscored the fact that there were varying opinions regarding deferred payment. It also underlined the urgent need to address the issue for a solution acceptable to all. The majority of the members were of the view that the practice of discounting deferred payment undertakings ought to be recognised by the upcoming UCP, and that the Drafting Group should come up with suitable provisions providing for the discounting of a deferred payment undertaking. Clearly, the onus was on the Drafting Group to clarify the situation and, in all probability, place deferred payment credits on par with acceptances and payment letters of credit. The group was also expected to supplement the process by drafting an appropriate article to reflect the final position of the Drafting Group.

At the Dublin Meet in June 2005, 27 countries out of 37 voted in favour of incorporation of a suitable clause to allow discount of deferred payment undertaking. The next issue was whether to give the nominated bank the authority, of course at its option, to discount an undertaking that it has made by way of an acceptance – whether under deferred payment or not. In documentary credit operations it is the applicant who selects the beneficiary, and opts to do business with him. Consequently, the general opinion was that the risk of fraud too should fall on the applicant.

Accordingly, it was decided that provision should be made covering the authorisation of the nominated bank by the issuer to discount or purchase an acceptance or deferred payment undertaking. At the Dublin meeting what was left unsaid was how that clause was to be structured to reflect exactly what the members wanted. The Drafting Group felt that it was not as simple as saying: 'Deferred payment undertakings may be discounted'. A suitable way out had to be found.

In an attempt to come up with an acceptable solution, a article was drafted. It was later amended. The amended article provided that a nomination by an issuing bank of a nominated bank to accept a draft or incur a deferred payment undertaking *included* an authorisation for the latter to prepay or purchase an accepted draft or a deferred payment undertaking incurred by it. The draft of this article was presented to the Banking Commission at its meeting on 16-17 May, 2006 in Vienna.

UCP 600 contains provisions that authorise nominated banks to discount documents drawn under deferred payment letters of credit (in contrast with acceptance credits, no draft is involved in the case of deferred payment credits) and to purchase drafts drawn against them under acceptance credits.

1.8.9 Article 28 of UCP 500

Article 28 of UCP 500 ('Road, Rail or Inland Waterway Transport Documents'), under an all-embracing article, deals with three different modes of transport. Document specifications could differ for that reason. The issue being debated was whether to retain article 28 as a *single* article (as it already was) or split it into three parts thus creating three individual articles to cater to three different modes of transport. During the conferences in Asia, it emerged that no one felt strongly one way or the other. Right up to the Dublin Meet, despite an earlier request from the Drafting Group, no clear consensus surfaced on whether or not article 28 of UCP 500 should be split into three separate transport articles or remain as one article with a general provision covering all three modes of transport; with individual articles covering the differences.

National Committees were, again, requested to indicate whether they preferred three separate articles or one as is the case in UCP 500. Twenty countries voted for retention of one article to cover all three modes of transport. Seventeen voted for a split.

1.8.10 Article 30 of UCP 500

Article 30 of UCP 500 is titled 'Transport Documents issued by Freight Forwarders'. The article states in essence that transport documents issued by freight forwarders were acceptable to banks as would transport documents issued by anyone else, as long as the issuer had signed as required by the relevant transport articles, i.e., as carrier, master, owner, multimodal transport operator or as agent of the carrier, master, owner or multimodal transport operator.

Article 30 was introduced only in UCP 500. This was done since some of the banks were not willing to accept transport documents issued by any entity acting in a capacity authorised by the UCP in instances where it also conducted its business as a forwarding agent. This approach on the part of the concerned banks was based on a misunderstanding. In reality, the UCP never did keep out of its purview transport documents merely because one of the businesses, or even the main business, of the issuer happened to be that of a forwarding agent. Rather, the UCP had always simply required that the issuer should be acting in the appropriate capacity when it issued the transport document.

The transport articles in the revised draft of UCP 600 ensured that it was so. The new draft transport articles were accordingly structured in an inclusive manner. The relevant articles did not distinguish between who the issuer was. A freight forwarder issuing a bill of lading and signing as agent of a carrier or as carrier was effectively covered in the new draft. The revised clauses enabled freight forwarders to issue bills of lading. Consequently, there was no justification to retain article 30 in the new version of the UCP. It became superfluous. At the Asia Annual Surveys too, most agreed that this article could be dropped altogether.

Thus, the Drafting Group was keen to delete article 30. The freight forwarders were not. They vehemently objected to the proposal. They feared that if the revised UCP made no specific reference to transport documents issued by freight forwarders, documents originated by them were likely to face problems. National Committees were requested to indicate if they disagreed with the proposal of no equivalent of article 30 (UCP 500) in the next UCP.

At the Dublin Meet, 30 countries voted for removal of article 30 (UCP 500) with seven voting for its retention. Currently whilst there is no equivalent for article 30 (UCP 500) in UCP 600, a reference to the issuance of transport documents by parties other than the carrier, owner, master or charterer has been included[36], specifically at the request of the freight forwarding industry since they

---

[36] Article 14.i, UCP 600 states, 'A transport document may be issued by any party other than a carrier, owner, master or charterer provided that the transport document meets the requirements of articles 19, 20, 21, 22, 23, or 24 of these rules.'

were concerned that the absence of an equivalent article in UCP 600 could invoke unnecessary refusals by banks.[37]

1.9 New articles for UCP 600

Though the Drafting Group was primarily engaged in a review of the 49 articles of UCP 500, the National Committees were also requested to indicate if they desired any new articles for incorporation into UCP 600.

Seventeen countries indicated no need for any new article. Other countries offered suggestions for inclusion of articles on the following subjects:

i. Corrections/Alterations

ii. Recourse

iii. Documents of title

iv. Inoperative LCs

v. Participations

vi. Linkage

vii. Jurisdiction

viii. Endorsements

ix. Revolving credits

---

[37] Commission on Banking Technique and Practice, meeting on Monday, 24 October and Tuesday, 25 October 2005, Paris, France.

x. Transfer by operation of law

xi. Good faith

xii. Language

xiii. Forwarder type documents

As was customary, the proposals were put to vote. Opinion was sought regarding which of these were to be included in UCP 600. Suggestions were also invited on new topics. Of the countries that responded, no single proposal received more than one-third support. As to whether there were any ideas for new articles, 17 countries said there was no need. Thus, there was no clear consensus for inclusion of one or more of the subjects or for the new ones. As a result, the proposals were dropped without further deliberations. (It may, incidentally, be noted that some of these issues have been addressed in the ISBP.)

1.10 The other important issues

Apart from the nine 'key issues' that were the subject of intensive deliberations at various meetings of the ICC, three other topics that also needed to be discussed at this point - and without a reference to which this discourse would not be complete - were:

a. UCP 500 articles or articles that have not found a mention in UCP 600,

b. Articles or topics that were not there in UCP 500, and appear for the first time ever in UCP 600.

c. Miscellaneous issues reviewed by the Drafting Group.

Brief discussions on these are presented in the following sections.

1.11 UCP 500 articles excluded from UCP 600

1.11.1 The articles excluded in UCP 600

The contents of the following articles, forming a part of UCP 500, did not find a place in UCP 600. The articles were as follows:

a. UCP 500 article 5: Instructions to Issue/Amend Credits (except article 5 (a)(i) incorporated into UCP 600).

b. UCP 500 article 12: Incomplete or Unclear Instructions.

c. UCP 500 article 8: Revocable credits.

d. UCP 500, article 14 (f): Discrepant Documents and Notice.

e. UCP 500 article 33: Freight Payable/Prepaid Transport Documents.

f. UCP 500 article 38: Other Documents – requirements excluded.

g. UCP 500, article 42 (c): Expiry Date and Place for Presentation of Documents.

h. UCP 500, article 46 (a): General Expressions as to Dates for Shipment.

1.11.2 Reasons for exclusion of these articles

The reasons for the exclusion of these articles from UCP 600 are explained as under in the same order as they are listed above. The first two articles are jointly reviewed as stated below:

i. *UCP 500 article 5: Instructions to Issue/Amend Credits, and*

ii. *UCP 500 article 12: Incomplete or Unclear Instructions.*

These two articles were essentially advisory in nature. The instructions contained therein were also general in nature. They could not, by any stretch of imagination, be termed as specific or categorised as 'rules'. Actually, one need hardly be told that instructions to issue or amend a credit, or the credit itself, should be 'complete and precise'. Moreover, there is no way to determine or define 'excessive detail' (UCP 500 article 5.a.i), no yardstick to judge when instructions failed the test of being 'clear and precise' (article 5.a). These 'rules', if they could at all be termed as such, were non-specific, and indeterminate – therefore not possible to implement internationally, across the board.

Even after these views were expressed, five countries wanted the UCP 500 article 5 reinserted in the revised UCP. Another five wanted article 12 to be retained in the revised version[38]. However, the majority view was that the contents of these articles should be accepted as good banking practice though they could not be translated into 'rules'. Finally, these articles were excluded from UCP 600.

i. *UCP 500 article 8*

Owing to the uncertainties inherent in the use of revocable credits, their use has progressively diminished worldwide. Recognising this trend, the Drafting Group decided early on that revocable credits would be excluded from UCP 600. Therefore, there is neither any equivalent of UCP 500 article 8 (Revocation of a Credit) nor the condition stipulated in article 6.b that, 'The Credit, therefore, should clearly indicate whether it is revocable or irrevocable' included in UCP 600'.

UCP 600 deals only with irrevocable credits. By its very definition, all credits would henceforth be *irrevocable* when issued. However, to issue a revocable credit (under UCP 600) a bank or issuer could always 'expressly modify or exclude' the applicable terms of UCP 600. The issuer of the credit would need to incorporate the full terms of the revocability conditions into the letter of credit, or better still, (if all parties agreed) could issue the credit subject to UCP 500 since it provides for Revocable Credits.

---

[38] Commission on Banking Technique and Practice, meeting on 24 and 25 October 2005, Paris, France.

(Wonder who in his right mind would ask for a revocable credit!)

ii. *UCP 500, article 14 (f)*

The matter of negotiation or payment of funds 'under reserve' or against indemnity is an arrangement between the nominated bank and the beneficiary. If, upon being informed that documents were non-compliant, the nominated bank decided to fall back on the beneficiary for recovery of funds paid earlier (under the reserve or indemnity), then the matter was purely between the negotiating bank and the presenter. The UCP had no reason to be concerned with such arrangements. There appeared no justification why payments under such arrangements should form a part of the rules of the UCP.

iii. *UCP 500 article 33*

Apart from the last sentence of article 33(b) and the substantive content of article 33(d), the remainder of this article was deemed to be unnecessary.

iv. *UCP 500 article 38*

A decision was also taken to exclude the requirements specified in UCP 500 article 38 titled 'Other Documents' viz.:

> 'If a Credit calls for an attestation or certification of weight in the case of transport other than by sea, banks will accept a weight stamp or declaration of weight which appears to have been superimposed on the transport document by the carrier or his agent

unless the Credit specifically stipulates that the attestation or certification of weight must be by means of a separate document.'

v. *UCP 500, article 42 (c)*

LCs being issued with validity stated to be 'for one month', 'for six months', etc., have become rare in practice. The SWIFT MT7XX series also requires an explicit expiry date, not a general statement of intent as to the intended date or period. General opinion was in favour of dropping this item since the article had lost its practical utility and relevance.

vi. *UCP 500, article 46 (a)*

Each of the transport articles in UCP 600 now indicates a statement of what is deemed to be the date of shipment[39]. Therefore, this article which provided an independent definition of the expression 'shipment' was considered unnecessary.

1.12 Articles in UCP 600 not present in UCP 500

Articles that are new to UCP 600 are as follows:

(i) Article 2: Definitions

(ii) Article 3: Interpretations

---

[39] Date of shipment was defined also in the ISBP for each mode of transportation.

(iii) Article 9: Advising of credits and amendments

(iv) Article 12: Nomination

(v) Article 15: Complying presentation

(vi) Article 17: Original documents and copies

Brief background to each of the new articles and the rationale for their inclusion in the new UCP are provided next, in the order of their appearance in this section.

(i) *Article 2: Definitions*

This was long overdue. Rules and regulations, acts and statutory directives usually begin with a section on definitions or a glossary. Apart from maintaining consistency throughout a document, this simplifies the drafting of the texts that follow. At the meeting of the Commission on the Banking Technique and Practice on 24-25 October 2005 in Paris, France, it was recognised that for some of the definitions the Drafting Group had fallen back on the definitions in ISP 98 (contained in Rule 1.09 and elsewhere in that document). Though ISP 98 concerned standby LCs, some of the definitions could also be made applicable to commercial LCs.[40]

Now that the UCP has gone ahead and introduced this section on definitions, one may very well wonder why it had not been done earlier. The introduction of definitions

---

[40] In actual fact, some of the other articles in UCP 600 have drawn on ISP 98.

has helped to streamline the structure of the articles, do away with repetitions, add precision to the texts of the articles, thereby effectively *reducing* the length of several articles and the UCP in general, and improving its quality of presentation. One feels that these ought to have been numbered.

(ii) *Article 3: Interpretations*

UCP 500 also provided interpretations. But they were placed in the text in an unorganised manner. They cropped up everywhere in UCP 500, sometimes at irrelevant or unexpected places, more often than not in juxtaposition with the textual matter of the main articles, thus reducing their impact. Now that the interpretations have been brought together at one place to the beginning of UCP 600, under a single article, they can be referred to easily. This step has helped to clean up the articles themselves, their contents being more focussed and the presentation sharper than before. The only thing missing is their numbering for ease of reference.

(iii) *Article 9: Advising of credits and amendments*

Issue of a credit instrument, its communication to the beneficiary, advising an amendment, the process of its acceptance or rejection by the beneficiary and the rules thereon – they constitute a logical chain of events. Strangely, in UCP 500 though the rules for advising credits and amendments were included under article 5, subjects like advising or confirming banks' responsibilities with regard to amendments, acceptance or their rejection of amendments by the beneficiary and other relevant rules were included only in article 9.d (i) to (iv) – broadly (and misleadingly) titled ‘Liability of Issuing and Confirming Banks’.

In UCP 600, all matters related to advising of credits and amendments have been brought under article 9.[41]

(iv) *Article 12: Nomination*

The responsibilities and liabilities of a nominated bank have been brought out clearly through a single article, divided into three articles, offering convenience and improving readability.

(v) *Article 15: Complying presentation*

Along with the very significant introduction of definitions, this article, and the coinage of term ‘complying presentation', should be appreciated by all the users of the UCP as a significant and a most encouraging development. The coinage of this expression has reduced lengthy and repetitive use of a series of words. The new article on ‘Complying Presentation’ also fills an important gap in the UCP, since up to and including the era of UCP 500, there was no rule or a stipulation that spelt out in clear terms what a bank’s duty was once it had determined that the documents complied with the terms

---

[41] Similarly, the other topics are also arranged in their logical sequence.

of the credit. The duties and responsibilities had simply been *assumed*.

(vi) *Article 17: Original documents and copies*

Over a period of several years there have been a number of queries raised with the ICC Banking Commission as to the manner of determination, by banks, of what should be recognised as an 'original' document under a letter of credit and the necessity, if any, for such a document to be so marked. In response, the ICC Commission on Banking Technique and Practice had on 29 July 1999 circulated Document No. 470/871 Rev. dated 12 July 1999 titled 'The determination of an 'Original' document in the context of UCP 500, article 20(b)' to clarify the position of the ICC. The preface to the document states as follows:

> 'The clarification, which does not amend UCP 500, proved necessary because a 1996 UK court case, Glencore International AG v Bank of China, narrowly construed the meaning of 'original' in article 20(b) of the ICC rules. As a result, document checkers worldwide tended to take an overly conservative view of what constituted an original for the purpose of the rules and were often unnecessarily stamping documents 'original' as a precaution.

The ICC Decision follows closely on the reasoning of a more recent UK case, Kredietbank N.V. v Midland Bank PLC, which clarified the Glencore decision. The Lord Justice in the Kredietbank case said that the real intention of article 20(b) was 'to widen the category of acceptable documents', not to narrow them.

The ICC Decision makes clear that 'Banks do not undertake to determine whether a document is original in fact'. It continues, 'The UCP neither requires nor permits an examination beyond the face of a document to determine how the document was in fact produced, unless the document was produced by a bank, e.g. on a telefax, telex, e-mail or other system that prints out messages received by the bank.'

The essence of the clarifications provided in this document constitutes the backdrop to article 17 of UCP 600.

1.13 Comments on a few other topics

1.13.1 'Unless otherwise expressly stipulated in the credit'

The above expression, or expressions similar in nature and intent, was more the norm than an exception in UCP 500. The words were first encountered in article 1. Several of the articles also started with or included the expression. So much so that it became repetitive. The expression in article 1 of UCP 500 'binding on all parties unless expressly stipulated in the credit' now stands modified. Article 1 of UCP 600 states, 'binding on all parties thereto unless expressly modified or excluded in the credit'. The expression is, thus, a little more specific.

It shows the intent behind allowing for changes or modifications.

One of the countries had suggested that a specific reference should be made to the fact that certain articles could not be modified. The Drafting Group had not accepted this, since it believed that, 'it was up to the bank receiving the L/C to determine if it did not like an exclusion or new wording, and if not to either reject it or seek to amend it.' (Refer to ISBP 745, article 1 for more on this issue.)

1.13.2 Honour, Negotiation

All aspects of the term 'negotiation' have been discussed at length in this book. As far as this author is concerned, the jury is still out on this issue. In the meanwhile, the UCP has introduced a new term 'honour'. A few words about these two terms may not be out of place here.

'Honour' is distinct in meaning and application from the term 'negotiation' – both having been defined in article 2 of UCP 600. The term 'honour' construes *payment.* When a bank *honours* (of course, a complying presentation), it *pays.* Under the provisions of the UCP, all *payments* by a bank are *without recourse.* This is the precise distinction between the terms 'honour' and 'negotiation'.

Consequently, an issuing bank *pays*, or 'accepts' under a usance transaction with a concurrent commitment to '*pay* at maturity'. It *does not negotiate.* A confirming bank, on the other hand, may honour or negotiate. When it honours (for example, when it pays against sight drafts drawn on itself), it pays *without recourse*. When it negotiates, it does so with recourse, unless it has confirmed the credit.

The conventional usage of the term 'payment' often clashed with the interpretation of the same term when used in the context of the UCP and documentary credits. Replacing the term 'pay' with the term 'honour' is, therefore, a step in the right direction and is indeed welcome.

1.13.3 URR 525

The norms and stipulations contained in the Uniform Rules for Bank-to-Bank Reimbursement under Documentary Credits (ICC Publication No. 525) find a reflection in article 19 of UCP 500. The more convenient option would have been to add the contents of URR 525 to the UCP 600 version of article 19 of UCP 500. However, the ISP 98 Rules make a specific reference, in Rule 8.04 to 'Any instruction or authorization to obtain reimbursement from another bank is subject to the International Chamber of Commerce standard rules for bank-to-bank reimbursements'. Therefore, a separate set of bank-to-bank reimbursement rules was anyway required. There was no scope to open up discussions for a decision on whether to include them within UCP 600.

1.13.4 eUCP[42]

The eUCP was developed as a supplement to the UCP due to the strong feeling at the time that banks and corporates together with the transport and insurance industries were ready to make that 'leap' into the electronic world of document and data delivery. The hope and expectation that surrounded the development of the eUCP have failed to materialise into day-to-day transactions and its usage has been, to put it mildly, minimal. Owing to this lack of usage it was felt that this was not the right time to incorporate the eUCP into UCP 600. It will remain as a supplement, although in a slightly amended form to identify its relationship with UCP 600.

However, the pandemic that gripped the world since late 2019 has once again brought to the fore the importance of digitalisation. Issues like eB/L, e-documentation, e-presentations are being actively discussed at multiple forums. We have to wait and see what evolves from these deliberations.

---

[42] Supplement to the Uniform Customs and Practice for Documentary Credits for Electronic Presentation or 'eUCP' provides an update to the UCP to accommodate technological advances. The eUCP is not a revision of the UCP. It is a supplement to the UCP that, when used in conjunction with the UCP, will provide the necessary rules for the presentation of the electronic equivalents of paper documents under letters of credit. This electronic supplement came into force on 1 April 2002. It was later revised.

Table 1.1:

Cross-reference to some of the issues reviewed by the Banking Commission

Topics	Cross reference
Should the 'applicant' be defined in the text of the rules?	Defined in article 2: 'Definitions'
Should all credits be considered to be irrevocable?	Defined in articles 2 and 3.
What should be done about letters of credit issued by non-banks?	Refer to section 1.8.2
Should the question of drafts on applicants be addressed?	Refer to chapter 2, section 2.5.3.
How was one to treat drafts in general in the new rules?	Refer to chapter 2, section 2.5.3.
What should be done with regard to the term 'negotiation'?	Refer to chapter 2, section 2.5.6.

contd...

Topics	Cross reference
What about the situation where a credit was subject to a sight payment by a nominated bank that did not pay?	Refer to article 7.a (ii) to (iv), UCP 600. The issuing bank remains responsible and liable to honour at all times under a credit issued by it.
Should 'signing' and 'confirmation' be defined?	Defined in the ISBP and the UCP.
Should the words 'without delay' be defined in more detail?	Refer to chapter 2, section 2.5.5.
Should there be time limits for amendments?	Refer to chapter 2, section 2.5.4.
What is the effect of a non-operative letter of credit and how does it work?	Not a part of the UCP.
How should the rules attempt to clarify some of the problems raised by controversial court decisions, such as the *Banco Santander* case?	Refer to chapter 1, sections 1.5 and 1.8.8.

1.13.5 Issues listed under section 1.6.3

We had noted earlier that the following issues were submitted by the UCP Drafting Group to the ICC Banking Commission meeting in Paris on 10-11 May 2004 for discussion. In this chapter and the ones that follow most of these topics have been comprehensively reviewed. For the convenience of the reader Table 1.1 provides ready cross-references to some of the reviews and discussions.

1.13.6 About some of the other articles

A few words would be in order about some of the other articles of UCP 500. Contents of articles 2, 6, 9, 10, 20, 21, 22, 30, 31, 33, 34, 36, 46 & 47 were been merged or catered for in other ways within the text of UCP 600. Details of the changes effected will become apparent from Part Two onwards as the respective articles are taken up for in-depth review.

1.14 Conclusion

This chapter provided the background to the entire revision process. These included the initial considerations that prompted the revision of UCP 500, the process of identification of the issues for review, the key issues and the reasons for their being identified as such. In this chapter, we also took up the articles in UCP 500 that were not considered relevant for being carried over or continued in UCP 600, and reviewed the new articles that have been included in the revised version of the UCP. We simultaneously examined the reasons for their exclusion or inclusion. Without such an exercise, proper understanding of the significance and the implications of the articles of UCP 600 would not have been possible.

In the following chapter we take up and discuss in greater detail the major issues, the articles that caused the bigger headaches (the 'problem articles'), some of the other areas of concern, the reasons thereof, and understand how these issues were finally resolved and taken to their logical conclusion.

These form an interesting backdrop to what we see as the UCP 600 today. The process was not easy. But at the end of the day it must be said that the current version is a far better product and a huge improvement on its earlier avatar.

+++

CHAPTER 2

MAJOR ISSUES IN UCP 500

2.1 Preamble

In May 2003 the ICC approved the process to begin revision of the articles of UCP 500. In chapter 1 we examined some of the 'key issues' identified by the Drafting Group and the Consulting Group. The considerations that caused them to be identified as such were also highlighted. In the process, we had a close look at the issues that inspired the International Chamber of Commerce (ICC) to initiate the process of revising and replacing UCP 500 with UCP 600.

When the revision process commenced there were over five hundred ICC opinions and two ICC decisions in place. These opinion had arisen out of issues that had earlier been brought to the attention of the ICC Commission on the Banking Technique and Practice (Banking Commission). There were also some forty to fifty DOCDEX cases to go by. The process entailed review of each of the Opinions in order to identify it either as an *issue* that had surfaced due to change in practices in the areas of banking, transport, insurance, etc., or 'an issue that has arisen due to lack of clarity, understanding or substance within the respective UCP 500 article(s)'[43].

The third option was to consider a request to the Banking Commission for an Opinion as an isolated, 'one-off' instance which, since it was 'one-off', was to be treated as such and hence did not call for a fresh review of the case, nor for any modification or addition to the wording in the UCP as it existed at the time.

2.2 Articles of major concern

2.2.1 The seven articles identified

It will be recalled that immediately after the Task Force was created by the ICC to 'deliver recommendations as to the issues that needed to be considered in the shaping and construction of UCP 600' it made certain suggestions for the way forward. One of these suggestions was to urge a view on the seven articles in UCP 500 that had given rise to the maximum number (over 58 per cent) of all the ICC opinions. These seven articles identified were articles 9, 13, 14, 21, 23, 37 and 48. Even among these articles, article number 14 titled 'Discrepant Documents and Notice' stood out as the single item causing the maximum

---

[43] *The origins of the UCP revision* by Gary Collyer, *Coastline Solutions Newsletter*, July '06.

concern. This article had been the cause of most requests for an Opinion.

2.2.2 ICC note on discrepant documents

In response to repeated queries on this single subject, and in its attempt to clarify the process of examination (and refusal) of documents, on 9 April 2002 the ICC Banking Commission had issued a document (Document 470/952rev2) titled 'Examination of Documents, Waiver of Discrepancies and Notice under UCP 500'[44] to explain how the process was expected to work under UCP 500. The document dealt with issues associated with articles 13 and 14 of UCP 500, especially the liability of an issuing bank having sought and received waiver, holding documents at disposal, clarity of discrepancies observed and the discrepancies being contained within one single advice of refusal. The document is comprehensive in nature, and outlined in detail the various stages of examination, approval or rejection of documents presented under a letter of credit. A flow chart annexed to the note further helped to illustrate the process.

2.2.3 Article 48 on Transferable Credits

Another issue of immediate concern was UCP 500 article 48 on Transferable Credits. From the number of questions that had been posed, the Banking Commission concluded that there was confusion with regard to some of the

---

[44] Available at www.iccwbo.org

provisions of article 48. It also appeared that there were parties who were issuing transferable credits which contained conditions that went beyond those provided for in article 48. This article too had given rise to a number of opinions from the ICC Banking Commission. To address the growing problems with regard to article 48, the ICC Banking Commission had, on 30 October 2002, issued a document titled 'Transferable Credits and the UCP 500'. It was the suggestion of the Consulting Group that confusions with regard to article 48 be addressed while drafting the new UCP.

2.2.4 The Position Papers

On 1 September 1994 the ICC Banking Commission issued Position Papers numbered 1 to 4 'to emphasise the need to correctly interpret and apply UCP 500 article 9(d)(iii) - Amendments; article 10(b)(ii) - Negotiation; article 13(c) - Non-documentary conditions; and the related articles of articles 23 to 30 - Transport Documents'. The Banking Commission went so far as to categorically state that 'failure to interpret the articles as indicated, in future, should be seen as in violation of the principles of UCP 500.' A reference to sections 2.4 to 2.11 would show that the subjects addressed in three of these Position Papers were among those that had given rise to the maximum number of queries and opinions. With the introduction of UCP 600 where the issues were addressed, these Position Papers became redundant.

2.3 Other articles causing concern

Compared to the seven articles giving rise to and constituting 58 per cent of all the ICC Opinions, seventeen articles had resulted in either none or only one or two ICC Opinions. Since these articles had caused little or no problem with the users of the UCP or the Banking Commission, the natural temptation was to leave these articles untouched for the time being. The easier choice for the Drafting Group would have been to leave these less-problematic articles alone and concentrate on the major issues facing the Task Force.

However, a key point that had to be kept in mind was the fact that the approach to this round of revisions was to be holistic. It may be recalled that, as mentioned in chapter 1, it had been decided at inception that the revision would be technical in nature, not a line-by-line modification and correction. For example, one of the goals was that a conscious attempt would be made to introduce a more non-legal, user-friendly language. Another aim was to group together similar topics under distinctly separate articles and deliver them in a logical sequence. Changing the style and language of the UCP would necessitate changes in the construction of the articles themselves, even where such changes may not have been warranted initially. (Well, it must be said that the Drafting Group did achieve their objectives after a mammoth exercise.)

2.4 The problem articles

The 'problem articles', if we may call them so, identified were 9, 13, 14, 21, 23, 37 and 48. These articles called for a closer study to understand why they were termed so, the issues involved, and the response of the ICC to those issues. The study could also provide us with a background to the articles that finally emerged and found a place in UCP 600 as we know them today. The study would, therefore, serve as a platform for a better understanding of the articles in UCP 600.

The problem articles and the topics they relate to are listed in Table 2.1 for our ready reference:

Table 2.1: The 'Problem' articles

Article 9	:	Liability of issuing and confirming banks
Article 13	:	Standard for examination of documents
Article 14	:	Discrepant documents and notice
Article 21	:	Unspecified issuers or contents of documents
Article 23	:	Marine/ocean bill of lading
Article 37	:	Commercial invoices
Article 48	:	Transferable credit

Issues relating to these articles above are discussed in the following pages.

2.5 UCP 500 article 9: Liabilities of issuing and confirming banks

2.5.1 The issues in article 9

As had been stated very briefly in chapter 1, section 1(12)(iii), article 9 in UCP 500 was one of the longest, relatively more important, yet very jumbled up in its construction and focus. This article combined several critical issues under a single title and article number, with a somewhat misleading title 'Liability of Issuing and Confirming Banks'. It *was* misleading, because the title failed to reveal the fact that the article also included rules covering liabilities and responsibilities of the banks and beneficiaries with regard to *amendments*. Further, the term 'negotiation' appeared for the first time in this article, but without any definition or explanation of its meaning. This very same UCP 500 article introduced significant issues like:

a. Liabilities of an issuing bank,

b. Its responsibilities if the other (nominated) banks fail in their duties,

c. Negotiation without recourse,

d. 'Deferred payment',

e. The inapplicability of LCs made available by drafts on applicants,

f. The concept of 'additional documents',

g. Extension of confirmation to cover amendments,

h. Rules regarding partial acceptance of amendments,

i. Rules and procedure for acceptance or rejection of amendments by the beneficiary,

j. Implications of unaccepted amendments pending with the beneficiary.

Surprisingly, all these topics were somehow compressed into a single article, viz., article 9 in UCP 500! [45]

At the meetings of the Drafting Group the issues that came up for discussion with regard to UCP 500 article 9 are described hereafter. The respective descriptions also furnish the issues involved in some detail in order to provide the background and the contextual reference for better understanding and meaningful discussion of the concerned issues.

2.5.2 Liability of the issuing bank

The first of these concerned an issuing bank's responsibilities if documents were received, *not* from the bank to which the credit was restricted as per LC terms, but directly from the beneficiary or from another bank. Common sense would tell us that, in the normal course, if one of the terms of the credit was not complied with (presentation not in accordance with the terms of the LC), the issuing bank would no longer be liable to honour its

---

[45] In UCP 600, these issues have been segregated and covered comprehensively under separate articles.

commitment. However, the ICC Banking Commission made clear its position in this regard. Position Paper No. 2, issued on 1 September 1994, stated:

> '..... Failure by the beneficiary to seek and/or secure 'negotiation' from the Nominated Bank under a documentary credit which allows negotiation, does not affect the undertakings of the Issuing Bank and/or the Confirming Bank (if any), nor does it constitute non-compliance with the documentary credit terms, provided that conforming documents are presented by the beneficiary within the validity of the documentary credit ..... to a Nominated Bank or direct to the Confirming Bank (if any) or to the Issuing Bank.'

In other words, the issuing bank is at all times liable under its own LC (as long as its terms are complied with) irrespective of the performance of the other (intermediary) banks, including the reimbursing bank. This continuing liability has been brought out clearly in article 6.a of UCP 600 ('...a credit available with a nominated bank is also available with the issuing bank'), article 6(ii) ('A place for presentation other than that of the issuing bank is in addition to the place of the issuing bank') as also article 13(c). In order to invoke the commitment of the issuing bank (irrespective of whether an intermediary bank negotiates, honours, or it doesn't) the documents would have to be presented to the issuing bank *within the validity of the credit,* and it must be a 'complying presentation'.

2.5.3 LC available by draft on applicant

Articles 9(a)(iv) and 9(b)(iv) stated that '....A credit should not be issued available by draft(s) on the applicant. If the credit nevertheless calls for draft(s) on the applicant, the banks will consider such draft(s) as additional document(s).'

This stipulation in UCP 500 baffled many. Contrary to popular belief, this conditionality did not appear to have any intention to discontinue or prohibit the use of a (time or usance) draft. A draft is recognised in the Bills of Exchange Act (1882) (in India known as the Negotiable Instruments Act 1881). It has its uses, especially if its application is compared in the context of a deferred payment arrangements (without the protection of a documentary credit). A draft or a bill of exchange thus serves the purpose of an outright, unconditional promise to pay.

> 'If the beneficiary has a bill of exchange, he gets the Bill of Exchange law to fall back upon in case he does not get paid for. That is missing in a Deferred Payment Credit. In this case, if you do not get paid for, then you have to go through all the rigmarole of proving in the courts on the basis of your documentary credit operations that you are entitled to receive that payment at an agreed future date. Only then you can expect a favourable decision from the courts.'[46]

---

[46] *Proceedings of ICC Seminar on Revision of Uniform Customs and Practices for Documentary Credits*, October 1983, pp. 9, 32;

In case of non-payment on maturity, noting and protesting of a usance or a time draft, drawn on and accepted by the applicant, are the generally prescribed procedures prior to initiating legal action in a court of law (depending on the country concerned). For users of non-LC bills a usance draft plays an especially important role, as outlined earlier, in safeguarding the interest of the drawer.[47]

But a situation existed in UCP 500, as also within the Consulting Group, where 'a definite statement had been made that a draft *must not* be drawn on the applicant'[48]. A statement of such a nature appearing in article 9 of UCP 500, without any accompanying explanation, had left everyone confused and baffled[49]. Unfortunately, the confusion was allowed to persist.

The explanation, which had to be dug out from other sources, is simple enough. A (demand or a time) draft can always be drawn on the applicant of a credit. The requirement of this document (a draft), if included in the

---

and *Report of Seminar on Documentary Credits and Frauds in International Trade,* Bombay, November 1985, p.14.

[47] URC 522 article 24, provides for protesting thus, "The collection instruction should give specific instructions regarding protest (or other legal process in lieu thereof), in the event of non-payment or non-acceptance.

[48] Report of the ICC Banking Commission meeting on 24-25 October 2005 in Paris, France.

[49] Nothing has changed since then. Article 6(c) of UCP 600 continues to state that 'A credit must not be issued requiring a draft to be drawn on the applicant.' Nowhere does the UCP clarify this stand.

LC, would have to appear under 'documents required' (SWIFT MT700 Field 46A Documents required), in conjunction with other documents that are usually called for in an LC in the normal course.

The applicable situation is as follows. We know that an LC is a conditional commitment made by the issuing bank. The primary condition is about a 'complying presentation'. Article 10(a) of UCP 500 states that 'All credits must clearly indicate whether they are available by sight payment, by deferred payment, by acceptance or by negotiation.' The matter of 'availability' is a product of the UCP, for application by the issuing bank. From the time an LC is issued, irrespective of the drawee or the acceptor of a time draft, the issuing bank remains committed to honour or to pay. This has been stated unambiguously in article 9(a) of UCP 500, and reiterated in article 7 of UCP 600.

If the issuing bank is to honour its commitment under an acceptance credit[50] (which requires a time draft to be accepted and paid on maturity), the condition of *availability* of a credit cannot be made dependent on an event or stipulation that is *outside* the purview or zone of control of the issuing bank. The draft should, therefore, be drawn on either the nominated bank or the issuing bank.

---

[50] An LC available by sight payment need not necessarily stipulate a draft.

A reason for retaining this provision in the UCP is that some years back there were a number of banks that made their credits available by drafts drawn on the applicant. They believed that by doing so they had made the obligation to accept and pay fall directly on the applicant and not on the issuer. The practice went directly against the very concept and the basis of a letter of credit issued by a commercial bank. Hardly a credit any exporter would be happy with.[51]

The UCP does not prohibit the beneficiary from drawing drafts on the applicant. An LC could well stipulate accordingly, if so desired by the applicant and incorporated as one of the conditions of the credit. In that case, the credit should simply state under 'Documents required', 'sight draft on the applicant for ...(amount)' or 'usance draft for xxx days' sight for ...'etc. drawn on the applicant[52]. The issuing bank's responsibility would then lie in the acceptance *and* payment (in case of non-payment by a nominated bank) of drafts on maturity.

In conformity with this reasoning, UCP 600 has retained the provision. Article 6.c of UCP 600 states, 'A credit must not be issued by a draft drawn on the applicant.' Article 6(b) requires that a credit must state whether an LC is

---

[51] More on drafts in articles titled *An enigma called draft* and *What's draft got to do with it* in the book *Beyond Trade Finance* by the same author.

[52] Refer to SWIFT MT700 Fields 42C (Drafts at...), 42A (Drawee) and 42P (Negotiation/Deferred Payment details).

available, inter alia, by acceptance. It could have done well to complement this requirement by also clarifying that under such a credit drafts must be drawn on the nominated or the issuing bank. Unfortunately, the Drafting Group has chosen not to avail of this opportunity to clear the air in this regard.

The position, as it had always been, was as follows:

i. For credits available by acceptance, an issuing bank may stipulate that a credit issued by it would be available by draft - drawn either on the nominated bank or on itself.

ii. For negotiation credits, a draft need not be stipulated. The applicant and the issuing bank could still ask for a draft, but only under 'documents required'. In that event, it should be drawn on the applicant. It should not be drawn on the issuing or the nominated bank.[53]

iii. The LC could also stipulate a usance or time draft. Once again, it should be drawn on the applicant for acceptance and payment on

---

[53] The position has been clearly stated in ISBP, ICC Publication No. 681, which was redrafted *after* UCP 600 was released. Article 54 of the ISBP states, 'A credit may be issued requiring a draft drawn on the applicant as one of the required documents, but must not be issued available by drafts drawn on the applicant.' Do note the use of the word 'may' in the article, and its underlying implications. The significance of this redrafted article in the ISBP may still be difficult to appreciate fully unless it is accompanied by a commentary on the subject. (Drawing of a draft is addressed more fully in ISBP 745 articles B.8 to B.12).

maturity. The requirement of a draft (on the applicant) would appear as a condition for compliance under 'documents required' or possibly under 'other terms and conditions' (SWIFT MT700 Fields 42C, 42a, 46A and 47A). Under documentary credit operations, the issuing bank would continue to be liable to have the draft accepted by the drawee and paid on due date.

Articles 9(a)(iv) and 9(b)(iv) of UCP 500 stated that '….If the credit nevertheless calls for draft(s) on the applicant, the banks will consider such draft(s) as additional document(s)' presented under an LC. This stipulation was removed in UCP 600 ('additional document' was never defined anywhere in the UCP, or what was to be the standard of its examination). Therefore, a time or sight draft would no longer be categorised as an 'additional document'. The ambiguity[54] associated with the status of a draft as an 'additional document' was thereby removed. This document (a draft) was to be subjected to the standard of examination as described in article 14 and ISBP 745.

2.5.4 Amendments

In section 2.5.1 we had highlighted the fact that article 9 of UCP 500 encompassed several distinct issues dealt with through several articles, all of them unfortunately

---

[54] The UCP nowhere states *how* an 'additional document' should be processed, handled or examined.

squeezed into a single article viz., article 9. With regard to amendments the issues that came up for discussion are described hereunder.

a. The first of these issues concerned a method of notification of amendment(s) that imposed a time limit - not envisaged in or encouraged by the UCP. A few banks had started inserting a provision in their amendments and amendment advices to the effect that the amendment would take effect unless it had been rejected by the beneficiary by a certain date or within a specified period of time. In response to this practice, through Position Paper No. 155 the ICC had issued its strong disapproval of the wrong practice. The Group had to decide the manner in which this Position Paper was to be handled in relation to UCP 600.

b. The effect of an amendment received and advised by an advising bank to the beneficiary – but pending indications of acceptance from or rejection by the beneficiary up to the time of settlement under an LC – was to be determined.

---

[55] The Position Papers precede UCP 600. They were issued subject to their application under UCP 500. The views expressed in these Position Papers were taken into consideration by the Drafting Group while formulating the revised version of the UCP. After the implementation of UCP 600, these Position Papers were applicable no longer.

c. Flowing from these two issues, the extent to which article 9(d)(iii) relating to beneficiary's response to an amendment advice was required to be modified, to the extent necessary, prior to its incorporation in the revised draft, was to be decided.

The primary issue concerned imposition of a time limit for rejecting an amendment. A point of view was that a beneficiary should demonstrate a certain degree of responsibility by *responding* to an amendment advice received, by either accepting it or indicating a rejection, all within a *reasonable* time. Since an irrevocable credit could not be amended without the agreement of all parties to the credit, the onus should lie with the beneficiary to *indicate* which of the amendments it chooses to accept or reject. Otherwise, it became extremely difficult (and frustrating) to determine:

a. whether an amendment had been accepted;

b. whether an amendment was applicable or not to a particular presentation; and

c. which amendment applied to the next presentation.

Recognising the dilemma, the Drafting Group did make an attempt to change the text of the relevant article. It revised the draft to impose a provision in the new rules that the beneficiary (in all fairness) must provide an indication of acceptance or rejection. The National

Committees were not favourably disposed towards the changes proposed.

The status quo, therefore, continues to be maintained to this day. The beneficiary wouldn't still have to explicitly accept an amendment. He can simply present documents that comply with the original credit (or the amended credit). The negotiating bank would have to determine the actual position obtaining with regard to the amendment(s) vis-à-vis the beneficiary, by comparing the credit and its amendment(s) whether the documents comply with the original credit or the amended credit, and thus, by inference, determine which of the amendments have been accepted.[56]

2.5.5 Without delay

UCP 500 has used the expression 'without delay' quite freely. The expression appears at seven places in articles 7(a), 9(c)(i), 9(d)(ii), 11(a)(ii), 11(c), 12 and 14(d)(i) of the UCP. Some members of the Group wanted it to be removed from the UCP and replace it with a specified number of working days. A few others felt that the term 'without delay' should be disregarded, as were other

---

[56] The situation obtaining as on date does not offer any solution. For example, if, under a credit that allows part shipment, an amendment increases the available amount from US$100,000 to US$ 150,000, and documents are submitted for US$100,000, one wouldn't know at that point if the beneficiary has accepted or rejected the amendment. One would have to wait for the next submission (if it was forthcoming) or the expiry of the credit, to draw a conclusion.

terms such as 'immediately' and 'as soon as possible' because, like 'reasonable time', 'without delay' did not describe a definitive period. A defined period of time would make it easier for those who preferred things being in black and white, for example, those who scrutinise documents or the legal profession.

But the issue was, what would be that number of days? The question also was, what would the penalty be if the party did not act 'without delay' or within a certain number of days? It is a simple thing to impose a deadline where there is a clear 'penalty' for failure to comply. But, since the expression was being used in many contexts by a lot of people, the period could not be defined with exactitude. What then?

There was no clear solution to this. It was, therefore, decided to live with the term 'without delay', but with the expectation that banks would act in accordance with the intent with which the words were used, i.e., expeditiously. In the final version of UCP 600 the expression appears at six places.

2.5.6 Negotiation

The issue related to the difference between the terms acceptance, payment and negotiation. Article 10(a) of UCP 500 states that, 'All credits must clearly indicate whether they are available by sight payment, by deferred payment, by acceptance or by negotiation'. But since 1933 when the UCP was first introduced, negotiation had never been defined nor its difference with similar terms such as 'payment' or 'acceptance' (as a method of settlement) had ever been brought out clearly.

Hence, the issue that engaged the attention of the members of the Drafting Group was 'What should be done with the term negotiation'? A suggestion was that nomination by an issuing bank of another bank to accept a draft or incur a deferred payment undertaking should simultaneously include an authorisation for the nominated bank to prepay or purchase an accepted draft or a deferred payment undertaking incurred by the nominated bank. Further, as was the position obtaining at the time, negotiation was to include payment or agreement to pay against presentation; mere examination and forwarding the documents without committing to pay was to be excluded from the meaning of the term negotiation. Some of these issues have been discussed in section 2.5.6.[57]

In the end, the term negotiation was retained by a majority vote. A definition of the term was also included under Article 2 of UCP 600. In addition, the ICC introduced the concept of 'honour' which effectively replaced the term 'pay' and encompassed the settlement types, viz., payment, acceptance and deferred payment. The

---

[57] The term negotiation is analysed in depth in the articles (1) Negotiation: the concept, (2) Re-defining 'negotiation', (3) What is 'negotiation' and why it must stay in the UCP, and (4) Some random thoughts on the UCP. The articles are available in the book *Beyond Trade Finance* by the same author.

confusion in the minds of most about the specific meaning and proper usage of this term was thereby removed.

2.5.7 Court decisions regarding discounting of deferred payment undertakings

This issue is discussed in chapter 1, sections 1.5.6, 1.5.7 and 1.8.8.

2.6 UCP 500, article 13: Standard for examination of documents

2.6.1 The critical Issues in article 13

Article 13 of UCP 500 covered several critical issues and concepts including that of:

a. reasonable care,

b. inter-se inconsistency,

c. presentation of documents not mentioned in the credit,

d. reasonable time for examination of documents, and

e. non-documentary conditions.

Examination of documents entailed decisions on mathematical calculations, errors in typing, formats for dates, verifying maturity dates for time drafts, inconsistency in shipping marks, additional information in documents (in addition to those called for in an LC), transport documents that were consigned to the drawee against those issued 'to order'. The matter about 'reasonable time' was one of the issues that also required to be sorted out.

With respect to article 13, there were other related issues that had to be deliberated upon and resolved. The problems and questions that lay at the core of these issues are briefly enumerated in the following sections.

2.6.2 Definition of the term 'banking days'

Article 13(b) referred to 'banking days' with reference to the time limit for the examination of documents. But it did not define the term. What should be defined as 'banking days', was the question. In certain parts of the world Fridays were non-working days (bank holidays), but Sundays were normal working days. In some countries Saturdays (and Sundays) were days when foreign exchange transactions were not undertaken. In some parts of the world, Saturdays were bank holidays; yet in others, banks worked only for a part of the day on Saturdays but handled little or no foreign exchange transactions. Which of these were to be counted as 'banking days'? Further, should the short or truncated working days be counted as 'banking days'?

2.6.3 Dates of certificates

Should a certificate be dated? If dated, what should be considered as acceptable dates for the purpose of a letter of credit and in relation to shipment dates? Could a certificate be dated after the date of the LC, or of the date of shipment? In case the answer is in the affirmative (for either or both), should the *type* of certificate be qualified?

2.6.4 Reasonable time

For the purpose of defining 'reasonable time', what should be considered as the close of business hours?

2.6.5 Language in documents

How many languages would be permissible/acceptable? Should the advising bank be entitled to impose a limit on the number of languages in documents?

2.6.6 Mathematical calculations

On occasions, presentations include documents--especially invoices--containing lengthy calculations. For lack of any clarity, banks have been devoting considerable time in the verification of these calculations. Errors in calculations have also contributed to discrepancies and consequent delays. To what extent banks were to be responsible for verifying the accuracy of such mathematical calculations, was the issue here.

2.6.7 Goods consigned direct to applicant

How should the responsibilities of banks be defined where documents were received with discrepancies but goods were directly consigned to the applicant, making it difficult if not altogether impossible to have control over the goods? In such instances, discovery of discrepancies – and possible rejection of documents – would hardly be of consequence to the importer/consignee.

2.6.8 Documents not called for in the credit

Article 13(a) states that 'Documents not stipulated in the credit will not be examined by banks. If they receive such documents, they shall return them to the presenter or pass them on without responsibility' (presumably, to the issuing bank--author). The article, however, does not clearly state the position, the responsibility of, or the course of action for, the *issuing bank*, if and when it received documents forwarded to it that were not called for in the credit. The UCP contained no direction as to how the issuing bank was to treat or process such documents.

2.6.9 Last dates for presentation, negotiation etc.

Some credits stipulate a last date for *negotiation* of documents; others mention the last date for *presentation*. Yet a few others stipulate the *expiry date* for an LC. These variations had given rise to an impression that these dates differed in their implications. For example, the last date for presentation of documents need not necessarily be the last date for negotiation of documents. Similarly, the last date for negotiation could differ from the expiry date stated in a credit. The issue was as to how these dates should be reconciled in the revised draft of the UCP.

Apart from the issues highlighted in the preceding section, the task for the Drafting Group was to decide whether some or all of these issues:

a. were to be covered by UCP 600,

b. be dealt with through the ISBP, or

c. be addressed by both.

2.6.10 How these issues were resolved

We shall now take up the issues in the order of their appearance in the preceding section, note the response of the ICC and record the manner in which the issues were disposed of.

a. *Definition of the term 'banking days'* (ref. to section 2.6.2): 'banking day' was defined in article 2 of UCP 600

b. *Dates of certificates* (ref. to section 2.6.3): The matter was addressed through appropriate articles in the ISBP[58].

c. *Reasonable time* (ref. to section 2.6.4): The problem was addressed in an unusual fashion; the concept of 'reasonable time' was removed from the revised version of the UCP, i.e. UCP 600.

d. *Language of documents* (ref. to section 2.6.5): This had earlier been addressed through article

---

[58] Articles 13 and 14, ISBP (ICC 681). ISBP 745 articles A.11 to A.16.

26 of the ISBP[59]. The matter was allowed to stand as it had been.

e. *Mathematical calculations* (ref. to section 2.6.6): The issue was clarified in article 27 of the ISBP[60]. Only five of the forty national committees wanted to retain the term 'detailed mathematical calculations' in UCP 500. Further, there was no way to pin down what exactly could be termed as 'detailed'. The latter term was quite arbitrary. The proposal was, therefore, rejected. UCP 600 continued to maintain the position enumerated in the ISBP to the effect that banks were not required to verify the calculations themselves.

f. *Goods consigned direct to applicant* (ref. to section 2.6.7): One of the pillars of the UCP, article 4 of UCP 500 (article 5 of UCP 600), states that 'banks deal with documents and not with goods'. That position (restated in article 5 of UCP 600) remains unchanged. (Simply stated, banks should not be concerned about how the goods have been consigned, but with the terms of the credit and whether the documents presented complied with its terms; nothing beyond that.)

---

[59] Article 26, ISBP 645 (article 23, ISBP 681). ISBP 745 article A.21.

[60] Article 27, ISBP 645 (article 24, ISBP 681). ISBP 745 article A.22.

g. *Documents not called for in credit* (ref. to section 2.6.8): article 14(g) of UCP 600 now states that 'a document presented but not required by the credit will be disregarded and may be returned to the presenter.' Article 13 (a) which stated that the banks that received such documents may 'pass them on without responsibility' (obviously to the issuing bank) was an option expressly provided for in UCP 500. Since the UCP did not provide any direction as to what the issuing bank was supposed to do with such documents, did not spell out the issuing bank's responsibilities with respect to such documents or how it was to be examined (if at all), a view was required to be taken. The article was, therefore, modified and the provision removed from the UCP.

h. *Last dates for presentation, negotiation, etc.* (ref. to section 2.6.9): Taking note of the confusion in a few quarters, it was clarified in article 6(d)(i) of UCP 600 that 'an expiry date stated for honour or negotiation will be deemed to be an expiry date for presentation'.

2.6.11 Non-documentary conditions

With regard to this issue appearing in article 13(c), the National Committees opted to continue with the structure as obtaining at the time. The earlier provision has, therefore, been retained in UCP 600.

2.6.12 Data in documents

Article 13(a) had made a reference to documents 'which appear on their face to be inconsistent with one another'. Article 24 of the ISBP (ICC Publication No. 645) [61] asserted that 'the requirement is not that the data content be identical, merely that the documents not be inconsistent.' It still did not resolve the issue. The term 'inconsistency' was hard to define or pin down. In consequence, the interpretation of the term and its application themselves contributed to an increase in the volume of discrepant documents. The principle of inconsistency, therefore, had to be revisited.

The issue was resolved through a revision of the UCP. Article 14(d) of UCP 600 stipulated that data in a document:

1. should be read in context with the credit,
2. need not be identical to, but must not conflict with, data in any other stipulated document or the credit; and finally that

---

[61] Although the issue of 'inconsistency' between documents was underscored in article 24 of ISBP 645 (the first ever version of the ISBP), the concerned article was deleted in its updated version, viz., ISBP 681. The requirement of the *description of goods* not being a 'mirror image' continues to find mention under article 58 of ISBP 681, as it was earlier under article 62 of ISBP 645 or later, in ISBP 745 article C.3.

3. it is not a requirement for a mirror image but for a level of consistent data.

2.6.13 Other related issues in article 13.

As stated earlier, one of the matters for consideration was whether the UCP, the ISBP or both should be modified to accommodate the issues discussed in the preceding sections. It was noted that the following issues, viz,

i. errors in typing,

ii. formats for dates,

iii. multiple languages,

iv. the methodology for calculation of due dates,

v. inconsistency in documents with regard to shipping marks, and

vi. data included or incorporated in documents in addition to (i.e., over and above) what had originally been called for in a credit instrument

had already been dealt with through various articles of the ISBP (ICC Publication No. 645) which was current at that time. It was decided that the principles pertaining to these issues should continue to reside in the ISBP.

[This decision solved an immediate problem, and was acceptable to all as a solution. But it opened a crack through which many new 'rules' were later slipped into the next version of the ISBP in the garb of 'procedures'. Now we have procedures in ISBP 745 which are actually more like 'rules' and should have been in the UCP than in the

ISBP[62]. In fact, we also have dispensations by the ICC Banking Commission which modify the UCP rules, but are not in the UCP.]

2.7 UCP 500 article 14: Discrepant documents and notice

2.7.1 At the time this article in the UCP was taken up for review by the Drafting Group, it had attracted top honours and the maximum attention for the highest number of requests for an opinion. A mention of this fact had been made in the preceding chapter. This aspect worried the ICC the most, because the entire documentary credit operation hinged on documents, their compliance with the terms of the credit, final approval or rejection of documents and ultimately, settlement between the applicant, the issuing bank and the beneficiary. The standards, norms and procedures at every stage had to be correctly understood and properly applied by the party concerned. If the concerned provisions were misunderstood or were applied incorrectly – as seemed to happen – the purpose of this article would be defeated. To clear the air in this regard, the ICC Banking Commission issued a document

---

[62] Refer to article titled *What the UCP does not tell you about documentary credits* in the book *Beyond Trade Finance* by this author.

titled 'Examination of Documents, Waiver of Discrepancies and Notice under UCP 500'[63] which explained how the examination and refusal process were supposed to work under UCP 500.

2.7.2 This document was issued on 9 April 2002, just before the revision process was formally launched. UCP 600 article 16 titled 'Discrepant Documents, Waiver and Notice' replaces everything that had preceded it on the subject, and now reflects the principles of the ICC.

Article 16 includes additional options for the handling of discrepant documents. The words 'held at your disposal' have been deleted from the text of the new article. It also tackles the issue of certain banks providing a refusal notice that contained reference to releasing the documents once the waiver had been received and accepted, a position that was seen by the courts to be against the wording of article 14 of UCP 500. Thus, article 14 of UCP 600 improves on the relevant article in UCP 500 and the ICC document of 9 April 2002.

2.7.3 About the term 'reasonable time' appearing in article 14 of UCP 500, it finds no place in UCP 600 article 14. The maximum period for

---

[63] This document is available at the ICC, Paris website http://www.iccwbo.org/

examination, approval or rejection has also been re-set to *five* banking days instead of seven obtaining in UCP 500.

2.8 UCP 500 article 21: Unspecified issuers or contents of documents

2.8.1 Issuer of a document and its data content

The emphasis of this article was on the issuer of a document and its data content. If the applicant called for a document in the credit it was expected that the applicant would also specify who should issue such document and what it was expected to contain (its data content), since these would go to protect his interest. Unfortunately, the expectation often failed to materialise. Article 21 in UCP 500, therefore, provided that a bank would accept a document 'as presented' as long as its 'data content was not inconsistent' with other stipulated documents presented. The problem about interpretation of the term 'inconsistent' and its clear definition still remained out of reach (see section 2.6.12) but were urgently necessary.

2.8.2 Need not be a mirror image

UCP 600 article 14 titled 'Standard for Examination of Documents' was drafted to attend to this and other issues related to the examination of documents. Issues regarding 'data content' and 'inconsistency' were addressed through article 14(d) of UCP 600. The guiding principle was to be that the data need not be a mirror image, but at the same time should not be in conflict with data in other documents. A proposal that banks need not compare data between documents inter-se was shot down by the National Committees (thus continuing with scrutiny for inter-se 'inconsistency' between documents and the concept of data-conflict).

2.8.3 Date of document

Another issue concerned dating of documents. The subject had been adequately addressed in the ISBP, especially through its articles 13 and 14 (ISBP 745 articles A.11 to A.16). It was clarified in article 14(i) of UCP 600 that, unless the credit stipulated otherwise, a document may bear any date (including a date prior to the date of issue of the LC, or after the date of shipment) but must not be dated later than the date of presentation.

2.8.4 Name or title of a document

Concern was expressed regarding name or title of documents called for under an LC. The issues debated revolved around the following:

a. Must every document have a title?

b. Would the title of a document necessarily have to be exactly the same as that stated in the LC?

c. Would the lack of a title (but contents being clear enough as to indicate its purpose) be deemed as a discrepancy?

d. In other words, would titles projecting the intention of a document but not named exactly as in an LC serve the purpose?

Article 41 of ISBP 681 (ISBP 745 articles A.39 to A.41) provided the necessary clarification. The article stipulated that documents may bear a title as required by the credit, have a title similar to that stipulated in the credit or be untitled, but that its contents *must appear to fulfil the function of the required document*[64]. Application of mind thus becomes more important than routine processing of documents received.

2.8.5 Transport documents

With regard to transport documents two issues came up for discussion, viz.

a. the handling of non-transport documents (i.e. those not covered by articles 23-29), and

b. the difference in consignee information between a transport document and other documents that contain a 'consignee' field.

Both these issues had earlier been addressed in ISBP 645 (ISBP 745 articles A10 and A18). It was decided not to burden the UCP but to let the ISBP continue to deal with them (which was a mistake that's yet to be corrected. Refer to the article titled *What the UCP does not tell you*

---

[64] Therefore, if the title is as required by the credit, but the contents are not, the fact will be noted as a discrepancy.

about documentary credits in the book *Beyond Trade Finance*.)

2.9 UCP 500 article 23: Marine/ocean bill of lading

2.9.1 The key issues in article 23

UCP 600 article 20 is the revised version of article 23 in UCP 500. Both of them deal with bill of lading. Some of the issues that surfaced during the process of revision were as follows:

a. Disposal of issues raised through the ICC Banking Commission Position Paper No. 4 in relation to carrier name and signing.

b. In the new UCP, how should bills of lading issued via the internet be dealt with?

c. Ports of loading in L/C appearing as place of receipt on B/L and how to make them acceptable under the UCP.

d. Is a fresh look necessary at the definition of the bill of lading date?

e. The issue of an 'on board' date being before or after the date of issuance of the bills of lading.

f. The issue of authentication of alterations being carried out by more than one agent.

g. Suitable wording in the revised UCP to reiterate the fact that non-negotiable copies of transport documents need not be signed or separately authenticated.

h. A clarification that the outer limit stipulated for presentation of transport documents (being within 21 calendar days after the date of shipment) apply only to original transport documents (not to copies or non-negotiable documents).

i. Necessary wording in the new UCP to accommodate instances where ports of discharge in L/C appear as place of final destination on the bill of lading.

j. Should container yards and container freight stations be considered at par with the port of loading?

k. The use of ranges of ports or geographical areas and requirements for port of loading and discharge details.

The background to each of these issues and the debates surrounding them have not been discussed here. A reference to the concerned article of the UCP or the ISBP would help the reader to clearly understand the subject and the issues involved. The necessary information is furnished in the section 2.9.2 (next).

2.9.2 How the issues were resolved

The issues and concerns outlined above regarding the operation of transport documents (including bills of lading) were addressed as described below (the items appear in the same order as under section 2.9.1):

a. The seventh paragraph of 'Introduction' to UCP 600 clearly mentions the fact that all the four Position Papers issued in September 1994 were in respect of, and subject to their application under, UCP 500 and that they would not be applicable, and would have no effect, under UCP 600. (Actually, the required modifications were taken into consideration while giving final shape to UCP 600, making these Position Papers redundant.)

b. As long as the bill of lading met the condition of UCP 600 article 20, the manner of creation of the bill of lading was not considered as relevant. (In this context, a reference to eUCP may also be made.)

c. This issue was covered in article 20(a)(iii) of UCP 600.

d. It was clarified that the 'on board' date would be deemed as the bill of lading date.

e. The issue was addressed in UCP 600 article 20(a)(ii).

f. Clarified through article 94 of the ISBP (ICC 645)[65].

g. Article 95 of the ISBP (ICC 645)[66] had already covered this subject.

h. This is covered in article 14(c) of UCP 600. For the application of the 21-day limit, the article referred only to original transport documents. For obvious reasons, the 21-day limit did not apply to (non-negotiable) *copies* of transport documents.

i. This is covered by the ISBP, article 81[67].

j. The subject was covered in article 82 of the ISBP.

k. This is covered in UCP 600 but only in respect of Charter Party Bills of Lading (article 22(a)(iii)).

---

[65] Article 109, ISBP (ICC Publication No. 681); ISBP 745 articles A7 and A8.

[66] Article 110, ISBP (ICC 681). It may, incidentally, be pointed out that under each type of transport document, the ISBP has a sub-section titled 'Corrections and alternations' that addresses the issues specific to the type of transport document under reference. For example, article no. 86 is the counterpart of this issue that deals with multi-modal transport, article 130 for a charter party B/L, article 152 for air transport document, and so on. ISBP 745 article A31.b took care of this issue in a simpler manner by stating, "Copies of documents need not be signed nor dated."

[67] Articles 98 to 100 of ISBP, Publication No. 681. ISBP 745 has a separate section titled "Place of final destination, port of discharge or airport of destination" for each mode of transport.

2.10 UCP 500 article 37: Commercial invoices

2.10.1 Issues with regard to invoice

UCP 600 article 18 is the revised version of article 37 in UCP 500 dealing with commercial invoices. During the process of revision some of the issues raised with the Drafting Group for their consideration are described briefly as under. Most of them related to the areas that were prone to cause discrepancies in documents.

a. UCP does not refer to the Incoterms rules. Whether or not any reference to it should be made in the new UCP?

b. The address details (viz., fax, phone, email details) of applicant or beneficiary were to be exactly as stated in the L/C or not?

c. A clear message in the UCP that the description of the goods need not be stated in exact terms, but one that corresponds ('corresponds' to be defined).

d. The manner in which goods should be described in other documents.

e. A suggestion that, where the credit covers more than one type of goods and only one type is shipped, a shortened description of the goods could be used in the invoice.

f. Issues relating to advertising material and goods supplied free of charge.

g. About the description of goods shipped, additional information or description that went beyond what was stated in the LC.

2.10.2 Response to these issues

The response of the Drafting Group to the issues and concerns outlined in the preceding section regarding commercial invoice were as follows (appearing in the same sequence as in section 2.10.1):

1. This is not a UCP issue but one for issuing banks to consider in the construction of their LC. The articles of the Incoterms rules also provide guidelines as to the manner in which the Incoterms rules should be used. (One may also refer to article 65 of ISBP 645, article 61 of ISBP 681 or ISBP 745 article C8. ISBP 745 makes no further reference to the Incoterms rules.)
2. This was covered in UCP 600 article 14(j). It may be reiterated that addresses may be different provided they were in the same country as that of the beneficiary or applicant.
3. The principle and text are that which are in UCP 500. (The articles of UCP 600 read with article 63 and related articles of ISBP 745 article C3 on invoices cover the issues extensively and adequately. A reference may be made to these documents for more information on the subject.)

4. This has been covered in article 14(e) of UCP 600.

5. This is covered in article 64 of ISBP 645, article 59 of ISBP 681 or ISBP 745 article C4.

6. The issues are covered in article 68 of ISBP 645, ISBP 681 article 64.b, or ISBP 745 article C12.

7. This is covered in the ISBP 745 article A34.

2.11 UCP 500 article 48: Transferable credits

Article 48 was the subject of numerous opinions and resulted in the ICC issuing a 13,100-word document titled 'Transferable Credits and UCP 500'[68]. Article 38 in UCP 600 reflects the main issues raised in the various 'Opinions' and in the document prepared by the ICC. The issues included adding confirmation to the credit being transferred, documents being sent to the transferring bank, definition of terms and refinement on the requirements for notifying amendments. The redrafted version now appearing as article 38 in UCP 600 should help to provide a clearer direction for the users of Transferable Credits.

---

[68] This document is available from the ICC website www.iccwbo.org. Being a lengthy document, it has not been reproduced in this book. Since it offers several clarifications on wide ranging issues concerning Transferable Credits under UCP 500, a perusal of this document is recommended. To what extent these were later accounted for in UCP 600 is not clear to this author.

2.12 From UCP 500 to UCP 600, what has changed?

In sections 2.4 through 2.11, we had a close look at the so-called 'problem articles' of UCP 500, the issues that gave rise to these 'problems' and their impact on the shaping of UCP 600. Having had a closer look at the changes, the rationale for and the modalities of the changes made, we may now be in a position to appreciate the improvements that were finally brought about. The 'changes' incorporated in UCP 600 may be summarised as follows:

1. The articles are fewer in number: 39 articles in place of 49 in UCP 500 (possibly for reasons below).
2. A whole new section of 'Definitions' under article 2 was added.
3. Another new, useful section under article 3 called 'Interpretations' was added to the UCP.
4. New terms such as 'honour' and 'complying presentation' were introduced. Their introduction greatly helped to do away with repetition, and simultaneously reduced the overall length of the UCP.
5. Interpretations of terms that lay scattered all over UCP 500 were collated, rearranged and brought together under a common article. These are now conveniently located right at the beginning of the

UCP under article 3 titled 'Interpretations'. In the process, all the other articles could be cleaned up.

6. In UCP 500 several topics were often included under a single (often misleading) article, incorrectly grouped, placed or classified. The issue was sorted out in UCP 600.

7. The topics and the articles are far better organised. They are sensibly arranged, appearing in a more logical sequence.

8. Legalese has been abolished. Plain English is now more the norm. Long-winded sentences have been done away with. The articles were completely redrafted to make the sentences short and simple, the language easy to understand.

9. Irritants in the UCP were removed: unbridled use of 'and/or' and uncalled for capitalisations were discontinued; the practice of a single article leading to never-ending, multiple articles was reduced to the barest minimum.

10. Articles with a negative stance were turned to positive statements and rules. The stipulations were more direct and specific in nature. The thrust is on what must be complied with, not on what should not be done.

11. UCP 600 is a stand-alone, independent document. All important issues and

developments since the introduction of UCP 500 were taken into account in this version of the UCP. Therefore, there is no further need to refer to a host of external documents to get a proper and correct understanding of the articles.

12. Certain rules, responsibilities and liabilities, practices and procedures under the UCP, obvious but never clearly spelt out, were framed to clear the air.

13. Existing articles were redrafted and new articles were introduced to remove ambiguities, clarify or reiterate certain key issues or to fill up gaps remaining in the earlier versions of the UCP.

14. Overall, the UCP is now more user-friendly and a far better product than its predecessor.

2.13 Wrap up

In these two chapters, we made an attempt to trace the evolution of the new UCP, the process of its transformation from its earlier version (viz. UCP 500) and the various stages of its progress over the three and a half years that it took to complete the process. We examined the issues – big and small, critical and on occasions not really so but discussed nonetheless with all seriousness – that were brought to the Drafting Group and the Consulting Group for their deliberation and disposal. It is hoped that these two chapters provided of the process, and a better understanding of why UCP 600 is what it is today.

Yet, the saga continues. Even after the major issues were discussed threadbare and the curtain drawn on them, there are several issues that deserve attention, and possibly, a more comprehensive deliberation. A few grey areas and lose ends also appear to linger, calling for review. These issues are critically analysed and presented in the book “Beyond Trade Finance” by this author.

+++

SECTION 2

ANALYSIS OF UCP 600 ARTICLES #1 to #39

This section presents an analysis of all the articles of UCP 600, beginning with article 1. The style used for the presentation of the analysis and comments follows the format below:

i. **Article**: The relevant article number and the article selected for review will be quoted.

ii. **Equivalent article in UCP 500**: Cross reference (if any) to the article similar in context, or closest in terms of its relevance as available in UCP 500, will be stated here.

iii. **Analysis**: Review of the relevant section of the article of the UCP 600 will be narrated here.

iv. **Comments**: Place for additional comment, background data and information of general interest.

Notes:

1. Cross references to articles in UCP 500 that are considered as 'equivalent' or source articles for the new provisions have been provided to the reader for his ready reference. The cross-references point to the articles which are near-equivalents, nearest to the meaning or are similar in context. This is because almost all the articles in UCP 500 have undergone significant changes during their evolution to UCP 600. The cross-references, therefore, have been furnished on a 'best effort' basis; they may not necessarily be exact equivalents.
2. Significant deviations, revisions, redrafting and so on have been analysed, commented on and appropriate comments or notes have been appended wherever considered necessary.
3. 'No change' means no (significant) change in meaning or interpretation when compared with its counter-part in UCP 500. However, any point worthy of note has been highlighted.

Analysis of the articles of UCP 600 follows.

ARTICLE 1: APPLICATION OF UCP

The Uniform Customs and Practice for Documentary Credits, 2007 Revision, ICC Publication no. 600 ('UCP') are rules that apply to any documentary credit ('credit') (including, to the extent to which they may be applicable, any standby letter of credit) when the text of the credit expressly indicates that it is subject to these rules. They are binding on all parties thereto unless expressly modified or excluded by the credit.

Under review: Article 1

Equivalent article in UCP 500: Article 1.

Analysis:

The significance of the UCP article 1 requires a bit of explaining. Like most of the articles of the UCP, it leaves a lot unsaid, its wide scope and connotation understated. A summary is presented in the following pages.[69].

The UCP represents the *uniform* customs and practice (for documentary credits). The emphasis here is on the very first word itself, viz., 'uniform'. The UCP brings on to a common platform the interpretations of the rules, standardise practices and terminologies in documentary

---

[69] For a more comprehensive analysis, refer to chapter 3, section 3.4 of the book "Letters of credit: Theory and practice" by the same author, and to his article *UCP 600 article 1: Reading between the lines* in his book "Beyond Trade Finance".

credits – irrespective of the users' location, language, background, culture, practice or procedure. The UCP may, therefore, be recognised as a *standardised set of best practices* to promote the smooth operation of international trade through letters of credit.

The words 'are rules', inserted after 'UCP', were absent from article 1 of UCP 500. The status of the articles has now been clarified. These articles being *rules,* not *laws* or statutes propounded by a statutory body or authority of any country anywhere in the world, whenever there is any conflict between the UCP and the law of the land, the latter would invariably prevail.

Article 1 states, "....when the text of the credit expressly indicates that it is subject to these rules." If the parties agree to subject themselves to the rules of the UCP this must be clearly stated on the face of the credit. Banks issuing LCs using SWIFT MT700 format should ensure that the appropriate code is used from the following options against Field 40E to expressly indicate the rules the credit is being subjected to, viz.,:

- UCP LATEST VERSION
- UCPURR LATEST VERSION
- EUCP LATEST VERSION
- EUCPURR LATEST VERSION
- OTHR

'They are binding on all parties thereto....' means that once the parties subject themselves to the UCP, the rules are binding on them *'...unless expressly modified or excluded by the credit.'* These words mean that any provision of the UCP *could* be modified or excluded altogether if the concerned parties so desire, even if a documentary credit did clearly state that it was issued subject to the UCP.

So, what *can* be modified? The answer is quite simple – to the extent that the UCP allows. Such modifications or deletions are covered (and protected) by the UCP. The protection does not extend to modifications *not* provided for in the UCP articles.

As with UCP 500, UCP 600 continues to be applicable to Standby Letters of Credit to the extent applicable. It is advisable to issue SBLCs under ISP 98 since it is specifically tailored for SBLCs.

Comments: None.

+++

ARTICLE 2: DEFINITIONS

For the purpose of these rules:

Advising Bank means the bank that advises the credit at the request of the issuing bank.

Applicant means the party on whose request the credit is issued.

Banking day means a day on which a bank is regularly open at the place at which an act subject to these rules is to be performed.

Beneficiary means the party in whose favour a credit is issued.

Complying presentation means a presentation that is in accordance with the terms and conditions of the credit, the applicable provisions of these rules and international standard banking practice.

Confirmation means a definite undertaking of the confirming bank, in addition to that of the issuing bank, to honour or negotiate a complying presentation.

Confirming bank means the bank that adds its confirmation to a credit upon the issuing bank's authorization or request.

Credit means any arrangement, however named or described, that is irrevocable and thereby constitutes a definite undertaking of the issuing bank to honour a complying presentation.

Honour means:

a. to pay at sight if the credit is available by sight payment.

b. to incur a deferred payment undertaking and pay at maturity if the credit is available by deferred payment.

c. to accept a bill of exchange ('draft') drawn by the beneficiary and pay at maturity if the credit is available by acceptance.

Issuing bank means the bank that issues a credit at the request of the applicant or on its own behalf.

Negotiation means the purchase by the nominated bank of drafts (drawn on a bank other than the nominated bank) and/or documents under a complying presentation, by advancing or agreeing to advance funds to the beneficiary on or before the banking day on which reimbursement is due to the nominated bank.

Nominated bank means the bank with which the credit is available or any bank in the case of a credit available with any bank.

Presentation means either the act of delivering documents under a credit to the issuing bank or nominated bank or the documents so delivered.

Presenter means a beneficiary, bank or other party that makes a presentation.

ARTICLE 2 (analysis)

Under review:

Article 2 in UCP 600 defining the terms 'applicant' and 'banking day'.

Equivalent article in UCP 500: None. This article titled 'Definitions' is a new concept in the UCP[70]. There was no similar article in UCP 500 to help bring all definitions together at one place. However, it would be necessary to read more than one article in the UCP (and sometimes the ISBP too) for a full understanding of a topic.

Analysis:

For the first time, 'Applicant' has been defined in the UCP. In a broader sense, though the *applicant* had always been part of the documentary credit operation, its specific role had never been explicitly defined in the earlier versions of the UCP.

The words 'banking days' first appeared in UCP 500 under article 13(b). But what exactly constituted 'banking days' had not been defined.

The expression 'Banking day' carries specific implications. For example, if a bank is open on Saturdays or Sundays, those days would not be considered as 'banking days' if, on those days, that bank does not conduct any 'act subject to these rules'. If no documentary

---

[70] Also refer to chapter 1, sections 1.12(i) & (ii).

credit business is done on certain days, for example, those days would not be 'banking days' for the purpose of UCP 600.

Comments: *Applicant*: During the process of revision and redrafting, a phrase had crept in stating that the applicant was not a party to the credit. This phrase was later removed, 'since it could be dangerous in that it could have affected the recourse to the customer with respect to reimbursement'[71]. In a proper sense, the applicant is still not a 'party' to the credit because the contract (the LC) is between the issuing bank and the beneficiary. The contract of the applicant is only with the issuing bank, not with the beneficiary. Every contract is separate (article 4 UCP 600). For more on this, refer to chapter 3 section 3.6.1 of the book *Letters of Credit: Theory and practice* by the same author (April 2020).

SWIFT MT 700 Field 50 (Applicant) captures the information with regard to the party on behalf of which the documentary credit is being issued. SWIFT has another Field 51a (Applicant bank) with the following definition, 'This field specifies the bank of the applicant customer, if different from the issuing bank.'

Definitions of transferable credit, transferred credit and transferring bank are placed under article 38 on

---

[71] Report of the meeting of the ICC Commission on Banking Technique and Practice, on Monday, 24 October and Tuesday, 25 October 2005, at Paris, France.

transferable credits. The Drafting Group felt that transferable credit was not a standard offering and therefore the article on transferable credits should be self-containing. Since definitions related to transferable credits were specific only to the subject of transferable credits and not applicable to any of the other articles of the UCP, their inclusion under article 2 was avoided.

ARTICLE 2 (analysis contd. ....)

Under review: Article 2: Complying presentation

Equivalent article in UCP 500: None.

Analysis: *Complying presentation* is a completely new expression introduced in UCP 600. The new term reduces the process of 'submission of documents that appear on their face to be in compliance with the terms and conditions of credit' – usually repeated in all the articles throughout the UCP – to just two words, namely, 'complying presentation'. Its introduction has helped to avoid the use of repetitive text throughout the UCP.

The new expression provides a hierarchy by which a document examiner is to determine whether or not the presented documents are complying.

Complying presentation thus includes complying with,

1. the terms and conditions of the credit;
2. the applicable provisions of these rules (the UCP 600); and

3. international standard banking practice (not limited to ISBP).

This definition forms the 'backbone' for a number of other UCP 600 provisions.

Comments: The introduction of this expression could be one of the main reasons contributing to the reduced length of UCP 600, the simplicity in its language construction and its structure.

ARTICLE 2 (analysis contd....)

Under review: Article 2 (Definitions): Confirmation and Credit

Equivalent article in UCP 500: *Confirmation:* Article 9.b; *Credit:* Article 6 and article 9.a

Analysis:

Confirmation: The effect of 'confirmation' by a bank has been stated in this definition. A confirming bank *honours* or *negotiates* (a complying presentation)[72]. When it 'honours' it *pays*; under the provision of the UCP, all

[72] Compare this with that of the issuing bank, which only 'honours'; it never 'negotiates'. The difference should be clearly understood and the implications appreciated. In its understanding is the key to the meaning of the terms 'negotiation' and 'honour'. A proper appreciation of the difference would help to clarify a large number of issues that underline the liabilities and responsibilities of an issuing bank vis-à-vis a nominated bank.

payments are *without recourse* to the beneficiary. Negotiation, on the other hand, may or may not be without recourse.

Credit: Meaning a letter of credit, is now defined as any arrangement that is 'irrevocable', thereby constituting a *definite undertaking* of the issuing bank. The *irrevocable* nature of a letter of credit is now fully established. This development may be compared with the provisions of UCP 500.

UCP 500 article 6(a) stipulated that 'A credit may either be (i) revocable or (ii) irrevocable'; UCP 500 article 6(b) required that 'a credit should clearly indicate whether it is revocable or irrevocable'. The situation now stands totally changed. In the era of UCP 600, even if there is no indication on the face of the LC, it would be an *irrevocable* credit instrument.

Comments:

In UCP 500 article 9.a defined an *irrevocable credit*. Under UCP 600 all credits are *irrevocable* (by definition) even if there is no indication to that effect on the face of the credit instrument. Thus, the relevance of article 6 in UCP 500 disappears completely.

It may, incidentally, be noted that in UCP 400 all credits were deemed *revocable* unless otherwise stated. In UCP 500, all credits were deemed *irrevocable* unless otherwise stated. Under UCP 600, all credits are *irrevocable* in nature, whether the credit instrument indicates to that effect or not.

Technically speaking, the advent of UCP 600 does not preclude one from issuing a revocable credit. (Who, in his right mind, would do that anyway?) For, the introduction of UCP 600 does not invalidate UCP 500. Under UCP 600, in order to issue a revocable credit, a bank or issuer would be required to 'expressly modify or exclude' the applicable terms of UCP 600. The issuer of the credit would also have to take care to incorporate the full terms of the *revocability conditions* into the letter of credit. Alternate, and the easier option, would be to issue the credit subject to UCP 500 (if all parties agree).

ARTICLE 2 (analysis contd.....)

Under review: Article 2 – honour, issuing bank

Equivalent article in UCP 500: None.

Analysis:

Honour: This is a new expression introduced in UCP 600. It essentially means 'to pay' (all payments being *without recourse*). This term effectively replaces the often used expression in UCP 500, viz., 'to pay, incur a deferred payment undertaking, accept Draft(s) or negotiate against documents which appear on their face to be in compliance with the terms and conditions of the Credit'. Honour is primarily used as a drafting technique in order to make the articles more readable. Repeated references in the UCP to any or all the three types of actions (depending on the type of LC in hand) have now been condensed into a single term, viz., ‘honour’, thus reducing the amount of repetitive text in the new UCP.

LC available by *honour* being not possible (since ‘honour’ covers three distinct modes’), ‘availability’ as an expression is destined to remain in use in the UCP for some time to come.

Issuing bank: No change has been introduced, only a clarification has been added. The definition clarifies that the issuing bank can itself be an applicant (‘on its own behalf’) for the same LC.

Comments:

A reference to any of the articles, especially article 9, in UCP 500 where the longer version of the term was used extensively, will bring home the advantage of the use of this simple term ‘honour’ in the articles of UCP 600. It is another useful innovation to make life easier for all concerned. Only one small point: The difference in meaning between the terms ‘honour’, ‘negotiation’ and ‘payment’, for some people, will take some time getting used to.

ARTICLE 2 (analysis contd.....)

Under review: Article 2 - Negotiation, Nominated bank, Presentation, Presenter

Equivalent article in UCP 500:

Negotiation: Article 10(b)(ii)

Nominated bank: Article 10(b)(i).

Presentation: New.

Presenter: New.

Analysis:

Negotiation:

a. It is defined as an act by a nominated bank. Since an issuing bank cannot nominate itself, an issuing bank can never be a 'nominated bank'. Therefore, 'negotiation' is an act that takes place only at the point of presentation to a nominated bank (any bank other than the issuing bank) when it decides to act on its nomination.

b. The concept used in the UCP of funds paid upon negotiation being considered as an 'advance' is new. Any passing of funds (or a mere promise to) 'on or before the banking day on which reimbursement is due to the nominated bank' is the key to this all-new definition of 'negotiation'.

c. Negotiation is possible for part of the invoice value.

d. Negotiation credit is not the same as a payment credit. ICC Banking Commission Opinion TA 569 states, "A letter of credit that is stated to be available with a nominated bank, by negotiation, should not include any reference to claiming reimbursement from a reimbursing bank or, indeed, any reference to the debiting of the issuing bank's account held with the nominated bank…."[73]

Nominated bank: Definition has been expanded to include the bank with which an LC has been made available.

Presentation: According to the definition, a presentation can only be made to the issuing bank or the nominated bank.

Presenter: The definition includes 'other party that makes a presentation', thus providing for presentations on behalf of the beneficiary. The beneficiary need not necessarily be the *presenter* under

Comments: *Negotiation:*

1. 'Negotiation' is defined as 'advancing or agreeing to advance funds' on or before the banking day on which reimbursement is due. Assuming that reimbursement is received on due date, as is normally expected to take place, purchase and

---

[73] Refer to chapter 5 section 5.8 of the book *Letters of credit: Theory and practice* by this author for more on negotiation credits and payment credits.

consequent payment of funds 'on the banking day on which reimbursement is due' can, by no stretch of imagination, be defined as an 'advance'. The definition should, therefore, exclude the words 'on or'.

2. An indirect reference in UCP 500 article 10.b.ii defines negotiation as simply 'giving of value' (by the bank authorised to negotiate). It was too vague to be of practical use or of help in defining the term. For example, if negotiation meant 'giving value', what was 'payment' supposed to mean?

The UCP does not fully explain these terms. For example, while defining negotiation, the reasons for insertion of the words 'drawn on a bank other than the nominated bank' has not been explained. (The explanation is as follows. If the draft is drawn on the nominated bank, then the LC is said to be available by *payment, not by negotiation*. The nominated bank is then said to *pay* – or, to use the term newly introduced in UCP 600, 'honour' – against documents, it no longer *negotiates.* As per the definition provided by the ICC, all *payments* are said to be *without recourse.* Unfortunately, these have not been explained anywhere by the ICC[74].)

---

[74] For a complete coverage of the issue of 'negotiation' and related issues, refer to chapter 3, Note No. 1.

ARTICLE 3: INTERPRETATIONS

For the purpose of these rules:

a. Where applicable, words in the singular include the plural and in the plural include the singular.

b. A credit is irrevocable even if there is no indication to that effect.

c. A document may be signed by handwriting, facsimile signature, perforated signature, stamp, symbol or any other mechanical or electronic method of authentication.

d. A requirement for a document to be legalized, visaed, certified or similar will be satisfied by any signature, mark, stamp, or label on the document which appears to satisfy that requirement.

e. Branches of a bank in different countries are considered to be separate banks.

f. Terms such as 'first class', 'well known', 'qualified', 'independent', 'official', 'competent' or 'local' used to describe the issuer of a document allow any issuer except the beneficiary to issue that document.

g. The term 'bank' includes, but is not limited to, entities traditionally known as a bank or other financial institution.

h. The term 'shipment' used in stipulating an earliest or a latest date for shipment includes expressions such as 'loading on board', 'dispatch', 'taking in charge', 'accepted for carriage', 'date of post receipt' or 'date of pick-up'.

i. Unless required to be used in a document, words such as 'prompt', 'immediately' or 'as soon as possible' will be disregarded.

j. The expression 'on or about' or similar will be interpreted as a stipulation that an event is to occur during a period five calendar days before until five calendar days after the specified date, both end dates included.

k. The words 'to', 'until', 'till', 'from' and 'between' when used to determine a period of shipment, include the date or dates mentioned, and the words 'before' and 'after' exclude the date mentioned.

l. The words 'from' and 'after' when used to determine a maturity date exclude the date mentioned.

m. The terms 'first half' and 'second half' of a month shall be construed respectively as the 1st to the 15th and the 16th to the last day of the month, all dates inclusive.

n. The terms 'beginning', 'middle' and 'end' of a month shall be construed respectively as the 1st to the 10th, the 11th to the 20th and the 21st to the last day of the month, all dates inclusive.

Equivalent article in UCP 500:

Interpretations - Appears scattered all over UCP 500.

'A document may be signed…': Article 20.b last paragraph.

'A requirement for a document…': Article 20.d.

Analysis:

Interpretations- General observation*:*

Although the article is new, most of the content is not new. Almost all these interpretations were available in UCP 500, but in odd places nested within several articles, sometimes unrelated. This fact would be amply evident from the analysis of the articles in this section, as well as of the remaining articles. These interpretations - scattered everywhere in UCP 500 - have now been brought together and arranged under a single article (Article 3) for the very first time, thus sprucing up the main texts of the articles themselves. In the process, repetitions have also been avoided.

A credit is irrevocable..: In article 6.c of UCP 500 the default option was '…in the absence of such indication...' (a credit was to be deemed as irrevocable); it is no longer so in UCP 600. 'Revocable' is no longer defined in the rules. From now on, for credits issued under UCP 600, no specific indication on the face of an LC is required or expected. 'A credit is irrevocable even if there is no indication to that effect in the credit'. This is the second place in UCP 600 where the irrevocable nature of an LC has been reiterated. (Also refer to the comments and analysis under article 2).

'A document may be signed…': Article 20.b of UCP 500 had combined the definition of 'original document' with this article covering mode of signing a document. The subjects have now been separated. No change in content.

'A requirement for a document…': The article has been shifted and placed under article 2 in UCP 600. No change in text, except deletion of the expression 'unless otherwise stipulated in the credit'.

Comments: None

Article 3 (contd…)

Under review:

a. Branches of a bank in different countries are considered to be separate banks.

b. Terms such as 'first class',…

c. The word 'bank' includes…..

Equivalent article in UCP 500:

a. Branches of a bank…: Article 2, Meaning of Credit

b. Terms such as…: Article 20.a

c. The word 'bank' includes…: New

Analysis: *Branches of a bank...:* In UCP 500 article 2 incorporated this interpretation under the title 'Meaning of Credit' - not exactly the right place or title for this subject. This anomaly has now been rectified.

In UCP 500 the words used were 'are considered as another bank.' The word 'another' was reviewed and considered to be not a true reflection of the situation. 'Separate' was chosen instead for the purpose of these rules.

Terms such as..: Article 20(a) in UCP 500 was modified to simplify the article. The total length was reduced to less than a third. The article was re-phrased to reinforce the fact that the definition should exclude documents issued by the beneficiary.

The word 'bank'...: This is a new provision brought about due to the removal of reference to 'parties'[75] used in UCP 500. The interpretation of the word 'bank' in UCP 600 takes into account the growing practice of LCs being issued by various corporates and institutions.[76]

Comments:

In all the articles, the text used in UCP 600 takes considerable pain to separately identify every entity – whether an issuing bank, an advising bank or a confirming

---

[75] Refer to chapter 1, section 1.8.4, on 'Parties'' or 'banks'.

[76] Refer to chapter 3, Note No. 2, 'When a non-bank issues a letter of credit'.

bank. This is a new and welcome development, absent in UCP 500, and illustrates the conscious effort by the ICC to simplify the presentation, be clear in meaning, and present an improved version of the UCP.

Article 3 (analysis contd....)

Under review: From "The term 'shipment' ...." to the end of article 2.

Equivalent article in UCP 500:

a. The term 'shipment' used in ....: UCP 500 Ref.: Article 46.a

b. Unless required to be used ....: UCP 500 Ref.: Article 46.b.

c. The expression 'on or about' or similar ....: UCP 500 Ref.: Article 46.c.

d. The words 'to', 'until', 'till', ...: UCP 500 Ref.: articles 47.a & 47.b.

e. The words 'from' and 'after' .... : UCP 500 Ref.: Articles 47.a & 47.b

f. The terms 'first half' ....: UCP 500 Ref.: Article 47.c.

g. The terms 'beginning' ...: UCP 500 Ref.: Article 47.d.

Analysis: *'The term 'shipment'...':* Marginal change in text, no change in meaning or interpretation.

'Unless required to be…': 'prompt' etc. were used in UCP 500, but only with reference to shipment. The text of the original article has since been modified and rephrased to expand its coverage, to indicate that vague terms such as these should be avoided in all applications.

'The expression 'on or about'…': The expression 'five days' nested within this article in UCP 500 was modified to 'five *calendar* days'.

'The words 'to', 'until', 'till', 'from'….': Reference to shipment dates and maturity dates are now segregated and clarified. The interpretation of these terms in this article is specifically with reference to shipment dates alone.

One need to be careful about the context in which these terms are being used. Slight textual changes reflect the difference in determining 'from' in relation to a shipment term against the term that determines the due date of a draft.

'The words 'from'…': In UCP 500, the terms 'from' and 'after' were used only once in articles 47(a) and 47(b) respectively, but only in the context of 'periods of shipment'. In UCP 600 the terms 'from' and 'after' have been interpreted twice, separately. It should be noted that in the immediately preceding article the two terms were interpreted with reference dates of *shipment*; in this article they have been interpreted with reference to maturity dates of *drafts*.

The interpretations of 'from' and 'after' were taken from the ISBP 645 (article 45)[77].

'The terms 'first half'...': No change.

'The terms 'beginning',...': No change.

Comments:

With regard to terms such as 'prompt', 'immediately' and the like, the Drafting Group had widened the scope to cover other applications, not just with regard to shipment terms. The Group had qualified this by saying that the words would be disregarded wherever they were used in a statement or similar applications.

Regarding the terms 'from' and 'after', the Drafting Group's opinion was that there ought to be two definitions, one in relation to shipment and one in relation to bill of exchange usage. The UCP was redrafted accordingly.

ISBP 645 article 45(d) had begun with the words 'The UCP provides no guidance where the words 'from' and 'after' are used to determine maturity dates of drafts...' etc. UCP 600 came into being thereafter. Consequently, after the ISBP was updated with effect from 1 July, 2007, the concerned article (renumbered as article 43.d) in ISBP, ICC Publication No. 681 began with the words 'UCP 600 article 3 provides guidance that where the

---

[77] ISBP 745 article A15 (shipment date) and article B2.d (maturity date.

words 'from' and 'after' are used to determine maturity dates, the calculation of the maturity commences.....' etc.

[The currently operative ISBP 745 article B2.d states, "The words "from" and "after" when used to determine maturity dates of drafts signify that the calculation of the maturity date commences the day following the date of the document, shipment or the date of an event stipulated in the credit, for example, 10 days after or from 4 May is 14 May."]

ARTICLE 4: CREDITS V. CONTRACTS

a. A credit by its nature is a separate transaction from the sale or other contract on which it may be based. Banks are in no way concerned with or bound by such contract, even if any reference whatsoever to it is included in the credit. Consequently, the undertaking of a bank to honour, to negotiate or to fulfil any other obligation under the credit is not subject to claims or defences by the applicant resulting from its relationships with the issuing bank or the beneficiary.

b. A beneficiary can in no case avail itself of the contractual relationships existing between banks or between the applicant and the issuing bank.

c. An issuing bank should discourage any attempt by the applicant to include, as an integral part of the credit, copies of the underlying contract, pro forma invoice and the like.

Under review: Article 4

Equivalent article in UCP 500:

UCP 600 article 4.a: UCP 500 article 3.a and 3.b

UCP 600 article 4.b: New

Analysis: *Article 4.a:* Essentially, there is no change from its earlier version in UCP 500. Terms such as 'honour' and 'negotiation' were introduced recently in UCP 600 under the title 'Definitions'. The text in the third sentence of this article which states '...undertaking of a bank to pay, accept and pay Draft(s) or negotiate and/or to fulfil....' was accordingly modified to reflect these changes and incorporate these terms. The section, therefore, now reads as '...to honour, to negotiate or to fulfil...'.

Apart from these, there is no change from the previous version in the meaning or interpretation of this article.

Article 4.b: This sub-section is an *addition* to the rules. Article 3(a) of UCP 500 stopped at 'any reference whatsoever to such contracts' being included in the body of the LC. Article 4(b) of UCP 600 goes a step further, uses very strong words to discourage copies of the underlying contract, pro forma invoice, and the like to be included as an integral part of the LC.

Comments: The directive in article 4(b) of UCP 600 comes as a separate article, presumably owing to its importance to all concerned. Attaching copies of pro forma invoice, agreement or contract only adds to the time required for the examination of documents and increases the probability of discrepancies being found in documents. If the credit is not carefully crafted, a bad LC would do nothing to protect the applicant against an unscrupulous beneficiary. Refer to chapter 8, section 8.6 of the book *Letter of credit: Theory and practice* by this author for a detailed discussion on the subject.

A nominated bank, confirming bank, or beneficiary should carefully consider whether it should act on such an LC.

ARTICLE 5: DOCUMENTS V. GOODS / SERVICES / PERFORMANCES

Banks deal with documents and not with goods, services or performance to which the documents may relate.

Under review: Article 5.

Equivalent article in UCP 500: Article 4

Analysis: Major change: 'All parties concerned...' changed to 'banks'. The fact is that only *banks* deal with documents, *all other parties* deal with documents as also with goods, services or performances. The modification reflected the fact that the focus of this article was on *banks* and not on (other) parties to a documentary credit operation. This article underlines two important aspects of a documentary credit, namely, (a) the documentary nature of an LC, and (b) the independent nature of the LC vis-à-vis the actual state of the goods (the underlying transaction).

Because the focus of the buyers and sellers is on the goods, where they decide to use documentary credits as their payment instrument, it should be made to clearly understand the principles of an LC, the UCP 600 and especially article 5 (that banks work with documents and documents alone).

Comment: The beauty of this article is in its brevity and simplicity. This article is one of the pillars on which the global documentary credit operation stands. Yet, strangely, since the introduction of the UCP in 1933, it took more than seven decades to recognise this anomaly in the drafting of the text of one of the most important articles of the UCP. Although it is a major drafting change, in real life it would have no effect on documentary credit procedures and practices.

+++

ARTICLE 6: AVAILABILITY, EXPIRY DATE AND PLACE FOR PRESENTATION

a. A credit must state the bank with which it is available or whether it is available with any bank. A credit available with a nominated bank is also available with the issuing bank.

b. A credit must state whether it is available by sight payment, deferred payment, acceptance or negotiation.

c. A credit must not be issued requiring a draft to be drawn on the applicant.

d. i. A credit must state an expiry date for presentation. An expiry date stated for honour or negotiation will be deemed to be an expiry date for presentation.

   ii. The place of the bank with which the credit is available is the place for presentation. The place for presentation under a credit available with any bank is that of any bank. A place for presentation other than that of the issuing bank is in addition to the place of the issuing bank.

e. Except as provided in article 29(a), a presentation by or on behalf of the beneficiary must be made on or before the expiry date.

Under review: UCP 600 article 6.a

Equivalent article in UCP 500: Article 10.b.i.

Analysis: UCP 500 article 10.b.i. began with the words 'Unless the Credit stipulates that it is available only with ...' but ended the paragraph with 'In a freely negotiable credit, any bank...'. Thus, the article itself was confusing in its structure, beginning with the description of a credit that was 'freely *available'* (say, by negotiation, acceptance or payment) but ending with the description of credit that was 'freely *negotiable*' – which implied that the credit was freely available *only by negotiation,* but not freely available by payment or acceptance. This was *not* the intention of the article.

The revised text in UCP 600 avoids confusion between the terms 'available' and 'negotiable' occurring in the *same* clause, the *same* paragraph. The revised article in UCP 600 now refers only to *availability* not *negotiability*.

The definition hidden within article 14.b.i viz., 'In a freely available credit any bank is a nominated bank' has now been brought to the fore by being placed against the definition of a 'nominated bank' under article 2 (Definitions) in UCP 600. This clarification helps to define and highlight the term 'nominated bank', especially for a credit that is freely available.

It is an essential feature of the UCP that a credit is *always, and simultaneously*, available with the issuing bank – irrespective of whether it is also available with another bank (viz., a nominated bank). But, up to and including the era covered by UCP 500, one had to interpret the various articles – mainly articles 9.a and 10.b.i – to arrive at this conclusion. This article in UCP 600 unequivocally reiterates this position and clarifies the issue.

This article also underscores the fact that, irrespective of whether a bank nominated under the credit performs its obligations or fails to do so, the beneficiary has recourse to the issuing bank for relief under a documentary credit as long as it presents complying documents to the issuing bank on or before the expiry of the credit (see article 6.e). The concurrent and concurrent obligations of the issuing bank are reflected in article 7 of UCP 600 (Issuing Bank Undertaking).

Comment: The continuing liability of the issuing bank had never been stated before in the UCP so unambiguously. Owing to the continuing confusion in interpretation, the ICC Banking Commission had earlier issued a separate note to clarify the position. This article of UCP 600 incorporates the earlier decision of the Banking Commission.

This article 6.d.ii could be useful, coming into play where the nominated bank is closed due to Force Majeure reasons like the pandemic of 2020 (see UCP 600 article 36).

ARTICLE 6 (analysis contd....)

Under review: Article 6.b

Equivalent article in UCP 500: Article 10.a

Analysis: No change from article 10.a in UCP 500.

Comments: Problem in distinguishing the inter-se difference, unfortunately, continues from that in UCP 500 and even earlier. The precise difference between the terms available by (sight) payment, deferred payment, acceptance or by negotiation is yet to be defined in the UCP. Definition of 'negotiation' in UCP 600 article 2 still does not clarify issues that have lingered over the last 70 years[78]. Banks still issue *negotiation* credits, though marked as being available only with the issuing bank or those available by payment. (See chapter 5 section 5.8 of book for more information on the subject.)

ARTICLE 6 (analysis contd....)

Under review: Article 6.c

Equivalent article in UCP 500: Articles 9.a.iv & 9.b.iv (part).

Analysis:

Stronger words 'must not' used in place of 'should not' appearing in UCP 500. Since an LC is the obligation of

---

[78] Refer to chapter 3, Note 1 for additional comments.

the issuing bank, it ought not to be made subject to an act of a party not having any stake in the operation of the credit per se – in this instance, the applicant[79]. For example, the operation of a credit or the issuing bank's obligations under that credit, should not be suspended in the eventuality that an applicant *refused* to accept a draft. Hence, if a credit was to be available by a draft drawn by the beneficiary, the availability should relate to the issuer of the credit alone but go no further. Hence, under such circumstances the draft should be drawn only on the issuing bank or a nominated bank.

UCP 600 avoids stating that in the event a draft on the applicant forms a part of documentation such draft was to be treated as 'additional document'[80].

Provisions regarding adding confirmation, amendment of LC (issue, advising, partial acceptance etc.) taken out of article 9.d of UCP 500 and placed under separate articles, titled as applicable, in UCP 600.

Comments:

The construction of the article fails even now, after yet another drafting revision, to convey the true intention of the ICC. The structure of the article does not appear to clarify or resolve what had always been the bone of contention, or the crux of the problem. Quite justifiably,

---

[79] Refer to sections 3.6.1 and 8.8 of the book *Letters of credit: Theory and practice* by Rupnarayan Bose (Notion Press, 2020)
[80] Refer to chapter 2 sections 2.5.3 and 2.6.8 for a review of the issues covering 'draft on applicant' and 'additional document'.

the objection of the ICC had always been to an LC being made *available by draft on applicant*. But a draft simply as part of required documentation was always possible and acceptable as a condition of a credit instrument (although this position had never been explained or clearly stated). The position was clarified in the ISBP 745 which was redrafted after UCP 600 was approved and released. ISBP article B.18 states, '(a) A credit must not be issued available by a draft drawn on the applicant. (b) However, when a credit requires the presentation of a draft drawn on the applicant as one of the required documents, it is to be examined only to the extent expressly stated in the credit, otherwise according to UCP 600 article 14(f)."

The inclusion of bills of exchange in documentary operations have created a storm in recent times. The uses of bills of exchange (drafts) is summarised under chapter 2, section 2.11.4 of the book *Letters of credit: Theory and practice* by the same author. Issues related to the use of drafts under documentary credits is presented in full under section 2.12 of the same book.

ARTICLE 6 (analysis contd. ...)

Under review: Article 6.d.i, Article 6.d.ii, Article 6.e

Equivalent article in UCP 500:

UCP 600 articles 6.d(i) & (ii): UCP 500 article 42.a

UCP 600 article 6.e: UCP 500 article 42.b

Analysis:

Article 6(d)(i): The article 42.a in UCP 500 has been reworded, simplified, made straightforward in structure and meaning. The important point to note is that the two issues 'place' and 'date' with regard to a presentation have been separated. In the expression 'All credits must stipulate an expiry date and place for presentation…' all references to 'place' have been removed. A passing reference to 'place' in UCP 500 article 42.a has been taken out from there, the section redrafted and inserted against a new article 6.d.ii in UCP 600.

The second sentence of this article 6.d(i) makes it clear that the terms 'presentation', 'negotiation' and 'honour' would mean the same thing as far as the cut-off date (expiry date) stated in the credit was concerned (also see comments below).

Article 6(d)(ii): 'Place' for presentation has been defined more comprehensively here. 'Place' has been expanded and re-defined in the context of

a. availability - of a credit for presentation of documents,

b. negotiability - under a credit that is freely negotiable, and

c. the issuing bank – a credit being always available with the issuing bank, and therefore (simultaneously) at the place of business of the issuing bank.

Article 6.e: In this article, the words 'by or on behalf of the beneficiary' has been added in order to accommodate presentations by a third party (for example, beneficiary's banker). Save and except this addition, there is no other change from UCP 500.

Comments:

Taken together, a conclusion can be drawn from the sub-sections of this article 6.d that an LC expires at the 'place' of the nominated bank OR at the *place* of the issuing bank – *on the same expiry date*. Unfortunately, this position has not been clarified in this article or anywhere else in the UCP.

It is unfortunate that SWIFT MT700 Field 31D has chosen to separate the "Date and Place of Expiry". This continues to cause problems for many, but both the ICC and SWIFT seems unconcerned. [81]

Additional comments on article 6.d(i): With regard to the second sentence of article 6.d(i), there was an increasing tendency in certain quarters to take advantage of a supposed ambiguity in the UCP. A conscious attempt was being made to distinguish between the last date for a physical presentation by the beneficiary and the expiry date for negotiation (or honour, payment) by the

---

[81] Refer to article "Availability and expiry under article 6, UCP 600" and "A critical analysis of ICC TA 717 rev2 (Worked out examples on 'availability')" in the book *Beyond Trade Finance* by Rupnarayan Bose

nominated bank of those same documents. The argument put forward was that as long as the beneficiary made a complying *presentation* to the nominated bank, the terms of the credit was complied with. By that logic, the last date for presentation did not include or extend to *negotiation* of documents, and therefore the bank that was supposed to negotiate, pay or honour could take its own time thereafter to do so.

For those who interpreted the provision of the UCP otherwise (and correctly), there was nothing in the UCP to fall back on to counter this (ill-conceived, mischievous) argument. The provision contained in article 6.d(i) of UCP 600 is, therefore, a statement that is very welcome indeed (if only SWIFT had not fouled up the pitch).

+++

ARTICLE 7: ISSUING BANK UNDERTAKING

a. Provided that the stipulated documents are presented to the nominated bank or to the issuing bank and that they constitute a complying presentation, the issuing bank must honour if the credit is available by:

   i. sight payment, deferred payment or acceptance with the issuing bank;

   ii. sight payment with a nominated bank and that nominated bank does not pay;

   iii. deferred payment with a nominated bank and that nominated bank does not incur its deferred payment undertaking or, having incurred its deferred payment undertaking, does not pay at maturity;

   iv. acceptance with a nominated bank and that nominated bank does not accept a draft drawn on it or, having accepted a draft drawn on it, does not pay at maturity;

   v. negotiation with a nominated bank and that nominated bank does not negotiate.

b. An issuing bank is irrevocably bound to honour as of the time it issues the credit.

c. An issuing bank undertakes to reimburse a nominated bank that has honoured or negotiated a complying presentation and forwarded the documents to the issuing bank. Reimbursement for the amount of a complying presentation under a credit available by acceptance or deferred payment is due at maturity, whether or not the nominated bank prepaid or purchased before maturity. An issuing bank's undertaking to reimburse a nominated bank is independent of the issuing bank's undertaking to the beneficiary.

Under review: Article 7

Equivalent article in UCP 500: Article 9.a.

Analysis:

UCP 600 article 7 - General observations:

Article 9 – probably the longest, and structurally the most complex article in UCP 500 – was simplified and completely redrafted. The various issues that this all-comprehensive article in UCP 500 dealt with have been split into three distinctly separate articles, viz.

(1) Article 7: Issuing Bank Undertaking,

(2) Article 8: Confirming Bank Undertaking, and

(3) Article 9: Advising of Credits and Amendments.

These three articles, redrafted and rephrased, bring out the responsibilities of the concerned bank(s) very clearly. The construction of these articles was further simplified with the introduction of the newly minted terms such as 'complying presentation' and 'honour'.

It should be noted that an issuing bank *honours*, it does not *negotiate* (when a presentation is 'complying').[82]

Comments:

Article 9 of UCP 500 was a combination of several critical and significant topics, all bundled under a single article[83]. Consequently, none of the critical issues received the attention or the emphasis it deserved. The reader also got confused, lost in the jumble of issues and topics. It became extremely difficult for an ordinary exporter or importer to properly interpret the articles or grasp the implications of the key provisions of these articles.

Thankfully, the problem was sorted out in UCP 600. Each of the issues is dealt with separately, comprehensively, and with considerable degree of clarity.

ARTICLE 7 (analysis contd....)

Under review: Articles 7.a(i) to 7.a(iv) of UCP 600

Equivalent article in UCP 500: Article 9.a(i) to 9.a(iv)

Analysis:

It was earlier emphasised that the relevant articles under UCP 500 were simplified, the individual subjects were segregated and separate articles, appropriately titled,

[82] Also refer to chapter 1, section 1.13.2 and chapter 3, Note 1 for additional comments on this subject.

[83] Refer to chapter 2, section 2.5 for comments on article 9 of UCP 500.

were created to separately address individual functions. Consequently, article 7 of UCP 600 begins with the issue of a documentary credit, and deals only with the liabilities and responsibilities of the *issuing bank*.

This article reflects the position of the issuing bank in three different scenarios (irrespective of whether a nominated bank acts or refuses to act under a credit) viz.

i. For sight credits: To pay if LC is available (at sight) with itself, or with a nominated bank,

ii. For acceptance and deferred payment credits: To accept a bill of exchange if the credit is available by negotiation of a usance draft (and pay on due date), or take up the responsibility of paying on due date under acceptance or deferred payment credits,

iii. For negotiation credits: To pay if the credit is available by negotiation, but the nominated bank does not (or refuses to) negotiate.

The main text of this article is lucid and requires no elaboration. Incidentally, it should be noted that a bank that has confirmed the letter of credit may or may not be a nominated bank.

Comments:

It is interesting to note the evolution of the UCP and the improvements in the drafting process. The following provides an interesting example. Even till June 2006, this section of the draft article of UCP 600 read something like below:

(a) A credit constitutes an irrevocable undertaking of the issuing bank - provided that the stipulated documents are presented to the nominated bank or to the issuing bank - and that the terms and conditions of the credit are complied with:

to honour:

i. if the credit is available by sight payment, deferred payment or acceptance with the issuing bank;

ii. if the credit is available by sight payment with a nominated bank and the nominated bank does not pay;

iii. if the credit is available by deferred payment with a nominated bank and the nominated bank does not incur its deferred payment undertaking or, having incurred its deferred payment undertaking, does not pay at maturity;

iv. if the credit is available by acceptance with a nominated bank and the nominated bank does not accept a draft drawn on it or, having accepted a draft drawn on it, does not pay at maturity… and so on.

Significant (and welcome) changes in approach to the final version, including use of the terms honour and complying presentation, appear to have come about only during the final phase of the revision process i.e., between July and October 2006.

ARTICLE 7 (analysis contd....)

Under review: Article 7(b), Article 7(c).

Equivalent article in UCP 500:

UCP 600 article 7.b: None in UCP 500

UCP 600 article 7.c: UCP 500 article 10.d (last section), and sub-section 14.a of article 14 titled 'Discrepant Documents and Notice'.

Analysis:

Article 7.b: It was emphasised earlier[84] that, by definition, all credits subject to UCP 600 would be *irrevocable* in nature. What is being stressed in this article is the irrevocable nature of a *bank's undertaking to honour*. An issuing bank is bound to honour from the time it issues the LC.

In this sub-section, the issuing bank's liability and responsibility towards a credit issued by it are reiterated.

The article also clarifies that an issuing bank 'honours', it does not 'negotiate' (Though the first lines of article 9(a)(iv) and 9(b)(iv) in UCP 500 erroneously stated 'if the Credit provides for negotiation – to negotiate without

---

[84] Refer to analysis and comments against article 2, Definitions (Credit).

recourse....', causing more confusion regarding the actual interpretation of the term 'negotiation'. The fact remains that an issuing bank *does not negotiate*.)

Article 7.c: Discounting of usance (acceptance) drafts now incorporated in the UCP.

UCP 600 article 7 addresses the issue that a nominated bank that has undertaken its nomination is entitled to be reimbursed by the issuing bank. This obligation is separate and independent from the issuing bank's obligation to honour a beneficiary's presentation. Reimbursement to the nominated bank by the issuing bank would fall due at maturity, whether or not a draft or a deferred payment undertaking was prepaid or purchased. (Also see article 12(b) of UCP 600 on the same subject.)

The 'independence' principle - that of the issuing bank vis-à-vis nominated bank, or that of a nominated bank vis-à-vis beneficiary – is enumerated for the first time in the context of a bank's undertaking under its own credit.

Comments:

A credit is invariably defined as an undertaking of an issuing bank. Yet, nowhere in UCP 500 had it been incorporated by way of a rule that an issuing bank was bound by the terms of its own *credit*. According to the provisions of the UCP (article 9.d.ii of UCP 500), the issuing bank's commitment was apparently only against *amendment*(s), if any, issued by it. UCP 600 corrects that anomaly.

Issues such as an issuing bank's liability to an LC issued by it, parts of articles 10.d and 14.a of UCP 500, plus the 'independence principle' – those that related to the issuing bank have now been eked out from some of the articles of UCP 500, as shown above, and brought together under a single article 7 of UCP 600.

ARTICLE 8: CONFIRMING BANK UNDERTAKING

a. Provided that the stipulated documents are presented to the confirming bank or to any other nominated bank and that they constitute a complying presentation, the confirming bank must:

   i. honour if the credit is available by

      a) sight payment, deferred payment or acceptance with the confirming bank;

      b) sight payment with another nominated bank and that nominated bank does not pay;

      c) deferred payment with another nominated bank and that nominated bank does not incur its deferred payment undertaking or, having incurred its deferred payment undertaking, does not pay at maturity;

      d) acceptance with another nominated bank and that nominated bank does not accept a draft drawn on it or, having accepted a draft drawn on it, does not pay at maturity;

      e) negotiation with another nominated bank and that nominated bank does not negotiate.

   ii. negotiate, without recourse, if the credit is available by negotiation with the confirming bank.

b. A confirming bank is irrevocably bound to honour or negotiate as of the time it adds its confirmation to the credit.

c. A confirming bank undertakes to reimburse another nominated bank that has honoured or negotiated a complying presentation and forwarded the documents to the confirming bank. Reimbursement for the amount of a complying presentation under a credit available by acceptance or deferred payment is due at maturity, whether or not the nominated bank prepaid or purchased before maturity. A confirming bank's undertaking to reimburse another nominated bank is independent of the confirming bank's undertaking to the beneficiary.

d. If a bank is authorized or requested by the issuing bank to confirm a credit but is not prepared to do so, it must inform the issuing bank without delay and may advise the credit without confirmation.

Equivalent article in UCP 500: Part of article 9.b.

General observations on article 8:

This article defines *confirmation* and devotes itself fully to the roles and responsibilities of a bank that confirms a credit. In UCP 500 article 9.b dealt with the subject of 'confirmation' including the role and responsibilities of a confirming bank. The same article also deals with several other topics[85]. In UCP 600 confirmation and related issues have been accorded their due place under an independent article.

In this article the Opinion of the Banking Commission has been incorporated; legalese abandoned, clauses made shorter and simpler – for all to understand the role and responsibilities of the confirming bank.

Refer to the 'comments' section against the analysis of articles 7.a(i) to 7.a(iv) of UCP 600 for related discussions. A segment of the draft of this article which was under consideration till June 2006 has also been quoted there. A comparison with the final version of this article will show the extent to which the language has been simplified and the quality of the presentation improved.

In this context refer to chapter 4 of the book 'Beyond Trade Finance' titled *The confusing world of confirmed credits*. This chapter points out a serious anomaly between sub-article 10(a) and 10(b) of UCP 600.

---

[85] Refer to chapter 2, section 2.5 for comments on article 9 of UCP 500.

Under review: Article 8(a)

Equivalent article in UCP 500:

- UCP 600 article 8.a.i(a): UCP 500, articles 9.b.i, ii & iii.a
- UCP 600 article 8.a.i(b): no direct equivalent in UCP 500
- UCP 600 article 8.a.i(c): UCP 500, article 9.b.ii
- UCP 600 article 8.a.i(d): UCP 500, article 9.b.iii.b
- UCP 600 article 8.a.i(e): no direct equivalent in UCP 500
- UCP 600 article 8.ii: UCP 500, article 9.b.iv (first sentence)

Analysis:

Articles 8.a.i (a) and 8.a.ii specify the *direct* responsibilities of a confirming bank.

A confirming bank *honours* (article 8.i.a) or it *negotiates without recourse* (article 8.a.ii). Essentially, honour is defined as to *pay* against (complying) documents; we know that when a bank 'pays' (as opposed to when it 'negotiates') it always does so *without recourse*[86].

---

[86] Refer to chapter 3, Note 1, sections 6.3 and 7.0.

The articles 8.a.i (b) to 8.a.i (e) reflect the position of a confirming bank that if a nominated bank does not act according to the mandate in a credit instrument. We have to remember that a nominated bank may or may not be a confirming bank.

In article 9.b of UCP 500 though the *definite undertaking* of the confirming bank – against the presentation of complying documents to '…any other nominated bank…' – had been established, in article 9.b.i the continuing undertaking of the confirming bank for failure *of any other nominated bank* (specifically, to make *sight* payment) had not been clearly stated. The position has been clarified in article 8.i (b) of UCP 600.

Comments:

From the text of the article 9.b of UCP 500 (excluding 9.b.iv), one would have had great difficulty in clearly appreciating the continuing responsibility of the confirming bank in case of failure of a nominated bank to act. Through the process of re-drafting and revamping the text of this article, this position has been brought out clearly, in plain English, and placed beyond doubt.

One may add that article 8 indicates essentially no change in the liabilities and responsibilities of a confirming bank from what was obtaining earlier according to UCP 500 article 9(b), but the presentation is far clearer.

ARTICLE 8 (analysis contd....)

Under review: Article 8(b).

Equivalent article in UCP 500:

UCP 600 article 8(b) : UCP 500 article 9.b

UCP 600 article 8(c): UCP 500 articles 9.b.i, 9.b.ii and 9.b.iii.b; article 14.a – Discrepant Documents and Notice.

Analysis:

Article 8.b: As always, a confirming bank honours (pays) or it negotiates. Two points should be noted. The first is that a confirming bank's obligations begin from the time it adds its confirmation to a credit. The second point to note is that the obligations (once it takes them on with its act of addition of its confirmation to a credit) are irrevocable. These facts also reflect the irrevocable nature of a credit under the UCP.

Article 8.c is restricted to a confirming bank's commitment to reimburse. This commitment covers

i. another nominated bank for having honoured or negotiated a complying presentation and forwarded the documents to the former, and

ii. reimbursement at maturity under an acceptance or a deferred payment credit.

It is important to note the new provision providing for purchase/discounting of acceptance draft or under a deferred payment credit (recall Banco Santander case[87]). Reimbursement by the confirming bank is due whether or not the draft or the DPU has been prepaid or purchased (discounted?) by a nominated bank.

Comments:

To reiterate, where a complying presentation has been made under the credit available by acceptance or deferred payment with another nominated bank, the confirming bank is committed to pay another nominated bank at maturity. This commitment is independent and irrespective of whether or not the other nominated bank has or has not paid upon presentation of documents payable at a future date, but before maturity (prepayment/discount) or has not paid subsequent to presentation of documents (purchased) payable at a future date, before maturity.

The undertaking of the confirming bank to pay another nominated bank as above is a separate contract from the contract the confirming bank enters into with the beneficiary.

The provision – covering reimbursement to a nominated bank by a confirming bank – in UCP 500 was placed under article 14(a) bearing the somewhat misleading title 'Discrepant Documents and Notice'. The subject has now been shifted and brought together at one place.

---

[87] Refer to chapter 1, section 1.8.8.

The terms 'honour' and 'complying presentation' appear to have greatly simplified the process of revision and redrafting of the original UCP 500 articles.

ARTICLE 8 (analysis contd....)

Under review: Article 8(d)

Equivalent article in UCP 500: Articles 9.c.i & 9.c.ii.

Analysis:

Articles 9.c.i & 9.c.ii of UCP 500 have been merged and simplified.

The term 'without delay' is retained but not defined further.

Comment:

The clause 'Unless the Issuing Bank specifies otherwise in its authorisation or request to add confirmation…' at the beginning of article 9.c.ii, UCP 500 being superfluous, has been deleted. The reason is that a bank requested or authorised to confirm a credit can only act within the parameters set by the terms of the credit, and not beyond them. (Refer to chapter 5, section 5.7.2 of the book *Letters of credit: Theory and Practice* by this author for more on adding confirmation and the related SWIFT MT700 format.)

+++

ARTICLE 9: ADVISING OF CREDITS AND AMENDMENTS

a. A credit and any amendment may be advised to a beneficiary through an advising bank. An advising bank that is not a confirming bank advises the credit and any amendment without any undertaking to honour or negotiate.

b. By advising the credit or amendment, the advising bank signifies that it has satisfied itself as to the apparent authenticity of the credit or amendment and that the advice accurately reflects the terms and conditions of the credit or amendment received.

c. An advising bank may utilize the services of another bank ('second advising bank') to advise the credit and any amendment to the beneficiary. By advising the credit or amendment, the second advising bank signifies that it has satisfied itself as to the apparent authenticity of the advice it has received and that the advice accurately reflects the terms and conditions of the credit or amendment received.

d. A bank utilizing the services of an advising bank or second advising bank to advise a credit must use the same bank to advise any amendment thereto.

e. If a bank is requested to advise a credit or amendment but elects not to do so, it must so inform, without delay, the bank from which the credit, amendment or advice has been received.

f. If a bank is requested to advise a credit or amendment but cannot satisfy itself as to the apparent authenticity of the credit, the amendment or the advice, it must so inform, without delay, the bank from which the instructions appear to have been received. If the advising bank or second advising bank elects nonetheless to advise the credit and any amendment, it must inform the beneficiary or second advising bank that it has not been able to establish the apparent authenticity of the credit, the amendment or the advice.

Under review: Article 9

Equivalent article in UCP 500: Article 7.a

General observation:

Credit and amendment to a credit have been combined in this article and given similar status. This article's equivalent in UCP 500 dealt only with credit and not with its amendment.

The expression 'without engagement' in Article 7.a of UCP 500 has been replaced by the actual position this expression was meant to convey viz., 'without any undertaking to honour or negotiate'. The limited liability in such a situation of the advising bank which is *not* a confirming bank is, therefore, clearly defined.

Although not stated in so many words, the article conveys a subtle message that a confirming bank advises a credit or an amendment 'with engagement'[88]. This is a very important point in documentary credit operation, but had never been clearly stipulated in UCP 500.

Under this single article, the entire procedure and the relevant guidelines relating to advising credits and amendments stand rearranged and grouped logically together. These critical issues had no separate identities in UCP 500.

ARTICLE 9 (analysis contd....)

Under review: Article 9(b).

Equivalent article in UCP 500: Article 7.a

Analysis:

Article 9.b: Subtle changes have been introduced in this sub-section.

As per the stipulations in the UCP, banks were always required to 'take reasonable care to check the apparent authenticity of the credit' it advised. However, no check or standard to *check* the 'apparent authenticity' had ever been prescribed.

A bank must now ensure that it 'satisfies *itself*' as to apparent authenticity. How that is to be done is up to the

---

[88] Refer to chapter 3, Note 1 for comments on the terms 'engagement' and 'obligation'.

respective bank to determine – but it must be done. A bank must, therefore, ensure that it has put in place the required procedure and necessary safeguards to establish 'apparent authenticity' of a credit. The revised draft brings about much more rigidity in terms of internal procedure of a bank advising a credit.

A few words regarding the expression 'the advice accurately reflects…': This article – as compared to its counterpart in UCP 500 - goes a step beyond 'apparent authenticity'. It extends the liability of the advising bank to communicate correct, full and complete text of what was originally received. The addition of the new clause is to emphasise the responsibility of the *first* advising bank to advise exactly (not in part but the complete text of) what is originally received.

Comments:

Advising of an L/C now casts two distinct responsibilities upon the advising bank:

a. authentication to establish the genuineness of the credit advised, and

b. to ensure that its advice to the beneficiary accurately reflects what was originally received.

It may be noted that the second stipulation is not totally a novel concept. The terminology has been introduced from ISP 98 (article 2.05 titled 'Advice of standby or amendment').

A question may arise at this point regarding the extent of the advising bank's compliance with this article. SWIFT format MT700 that's nowadays used universally to issue a credit contains more than one field viz. 49H, 78 and (in certain instances) Field 72Z that are not meant for the beneficiary. Several banks exclude these fields while advising the issue of a credit to the beneficiary. Are these banks violating the provision of UCP 600 article 9(b) while doing so?

In this author's opinion, the entire text of the credit, without mutilation, should be passed on to the beneficiary.

ARTICLE 9 (analysis contd....)

Under review: Article 9(c)

Equivalent article in UCP 500: New article/subject.

Analysis: This article 9(c) of UCP 600 formally recognises the role played by a 'second advising bank' for advising of credits and amendments, and explains the relationship between it and the (first) advising bank in documentary credit operations.

Comments: It is a variation of UCP 500 article 7(a). As with article 7(b), the additional responsibility to ensure that the advice 'accurately reflects' goes beyond 'apparent authenticity'; it emphasises the responsibility of the second advising bank to advise exactly and full text of what was received. By defining its responsibilities, the sub-section also defines the obligation and the responsibility of the *second* advising bank. (Refer to additional comments next, on 'second advising bank')

ARTICLE 9 (analysis contd....)

Under review: Articles 9(d), 9(e) and 9(f).

Equivalent article in UCP 500:

UCP 600 article 9.d: UCP 500 article 11.b

UCP 600 article 9.e: UCP 500 article 7.a (last sentence)

UCP 600 article 9.d: UCP 500 article 7.b

Analysis:

Scope of the articles referred above has been enlarged to add 'amendment and advice'. Advising an 'amendment' or 'advice' (see articles 9.e and 9.f above) are additions in UCP 600 to the text of the original articles in UCP 500 which, in article 7, referred only to advising a 'credit' and procedures related to a credit instrument.

Article 9.e: This article relates to the position of a bank if it *opts not to advise* a credit or an amendment (to the beneficiary).

In contrast, *article 9(f)* deals with an advising bank that *cannot satisfy itself* about the 'apparent authenticity' of a credit, an amendment or an advice.

Comment:

These articles recognise the *second advising bank* as an intermediary in the documentary credit process. These go on to define the inter-se relationship with the advising bank for advising of credits and amendments.

Article 9.f states that if apparent authenticity cannot be established, the advising (or the second advising) bank is required to revert to the originating bank. The last sentence states that '…it must inform the beneficiary or second advising bank…'. The pronoun 'it' refers to the first advising or the second advising bank or both?

Since the last sentence under reference starts with the statement 'If the advising bank or second advising bank elects…etc.' the pronoun 'it' immediately afterwards may also refer to the second advising bank. If that be the case, then '**it** must inform the beneficiary or *second advising bank*…etc.' is not feasible ('it' cannot advise *itself*). The instructed procedure holds good only if 'it' refers to the first advising bank, not otherwise.

According to this article, if the concerned bank still chooses to advise, *only then* the recipient (the second advising bank or the ultimate beneficiary, as the case may be) would get to know that the that apparent authenticity could not be established. If the credit, the amendment or the advice is not advised, there appears to be no responsibility on the part of the bank concerned to inform the intended recipient about the 'deficiency' (in the credit, the amendment or the advice), leaving the intended beneficiary none the wiser about such an issue.

In the light of the above, redrafting of the articles is called for.

ARTICLE 10, AMENDMENTS

a. Except as otherwise provided by article 38, a credit can neither be amended nor cancelled without the agreement of the issuing bank, the confirming bank, if any, and the beneficiary.

b. An issuing bank is irrevocably bound by an amendment as of the time it issues the amendment. A confirming bank may extend its confirmation to an amendment and will be irrevocably bound as of the time it advises the amendment. A confirming bank may, however, choose to advise an amendment without extending its confirmation and, if so, it must inform the issuing bank without delay and inform the beneficiary in its advice.

c. The terms and conditions of the original credit (or a credit incorporating previously accepted amendments) will remain in force for the beneficiary until the beneficiary communicates its acceptance of the amendment to the bank that advised such amendment. The beneficiary should give notification of acceptance or rejection of an amendment. If the beneficiary fails to give such notification, a presentation that complies with the credit and to any not yet accepted amendment will be deemed to be notification of acceptance by the beneficiary of such amendment. As of that moment the credit will be amended.

d. A bank that advises an amendment should inform the bank from which it received the amendment of any notification of acceptance or rejection.

e. Partial acceptance of an amendment is not allowed and will be deemed to be notification of rejection of that amendment.

f. A provision in an amendment to the effect that the amendment shall enter into force unless rejected by the beneficiary within a certain time limit shall be disregarded.

Under review: Articles 10(a), 10(b) and 10(c)

Equivalent article in UCP 500:

- UCP 600 article 10.a: UCP 500 article 9.d.i
- UCP 600 article 10.b: UCP 500 article 9.d.ii
- UCP 600 article 10.c: UCP 500 article 9.d.iii

Analysis:

No change from that obtaining in UCP 500 in any of the articles, wherever these occur in UCP 500.

Comments:

For the very first time, all matters relating to amendments (except the process of advising) have been brought under one roof. UCP 500 had no separate article, section, title, sub-title, or sub-section dealing exclusively with amendments.

As with UCP 500, the beneficiary retains the right to present documents under the original credit, even while an amendment could be pending his acceptance.

An example of the continuing potential problem area: Credit issued for $100,000 allowing partial shipment; no quantity, no rate or unit price stated. Credit later amended increasing credit amount by $50,000 to $150,000. Beneficiary presents invoice and documents for $100,000. Even after this presentation there is no way to determine if the amendment has been accepted or not. Unless there is a clear communication from the beneficiary of an acceptance or rejection of the amendment, one would have to wait till the next presentation (if any) or till the expiry of the credit, to know for sure about the fate of the amendment.

Article 10.c, last line: Suggest change for the line to read as '...the credit will *stand* amended.'

ARTICLE 10 (analysis contd....)

Under review: Article 10(d).

Equivalent article in UCP 500: New.

Analysis: Throughout the process of acceptance, rejection or a complying presentation, there was no provision to keep the bank from which the advice was received, or the issuing bank (and thereby, the applicant) informed or advised about the status of an amendment and the response of the beneficiary to it. This has now been taken care of.

Comments: Addition of duty, in article 10(d), on the part of the advising bank to inform the issuing bank of rejection, absent in UCP 500. It's a welcome addition to the rules, especially if presentation was still awaited.

According to article 10.c, in the absence of a specific communication from the beneficiary specifically communicating acceptance or rejection, (under these rules) only a presentation determines whether an amendment has been accepted or rejected by the beneficiary. However, after a 'complying presentation' (under, say, the original or the 1st amended credit - while a subsequent amendment remains outstanding pending acceptance) has been made, does this article stipulating that the advising bank inform the originating bank of 'acceptance' or 'rejection' still make sense? Should a separate advice need to be sent once again? What would be the implications or consequences if the bank concerned fails to comply with this provision, but leaves it to the originating bank (that receives the negotiated documents from this bank) to draw its own conclusions from the documents themselves?

ARTICLE 10 (analysis contd....)

Under review: Article 10.e.

Equivalent article in UCP 500: UCP 600 article 10.e:

UCP 500 article 9.d.iv

Analysis:

Article 10.e: Though there is no major change in this version of the article, the revised draft lends a more proactive and positive thrust to the rules. The clause 'will not be given any effect' in UCP 500 being somewhat vague in its objective, has been replaced in UCP 600 by the words 'will be deemed to be notification of rejection of that amendment'.

Comments:

To maintain a chronological sequence in the arrangement of the articles, shouldn't article 10.d have come *after* article 10.e?

ARTICLE 10 (analysis contd....)

Under review: Article 10.f.

Equivalent article in UCP 500: New

Analysis:

ICC Banking Commission decision, vide ICC Banking Commission Position Paper No.1 titled 'Amendments', referring to the 'unhealthy practice' among certain banks in setting default time limits, has now been incorporated as a sub-section in this article of UCP 600. (The Position Paper, therefore, stands withdrawn.)

Time limit restriction or default option for acceptance or rejection will be disregarded. (This provision was inserted with the specific aim to discourage attempts by some banks to change the rules by such means.)

Comments:

There is a serious logical error in the first three articles of article 10. The error is discussed in detail in an article titled xxx in the book *Beyond Trade Finance* by this same author.

+++

ARTICLE 11: TELETRANSMITTED AND PRE-ADVISED CREDITS AND AMENDMENTS

a. An authenticated teletransmission of a credit or amendment will be deemed to be the operative credit or amendment, and any subsequent mail confirmation shall be disregarded.

b. If a teletransmission states 'full details to follow' (or words of similar effect), or states that the mail confirmation is to be the operative credit or amendment, then the teletransmission will not be deemed to be the operative credit or amendment. The issuing bank must then issue the operative credit or amendment without delay in terms not inconsistent with the teletransmission.

c. A preliminary advice of the issuance of a credit or amendment ('pre-advice') shall only be sent if the issuing bank is prepared to issue the operative credit or amendment. An issuing bank that sends a pre-advice is irrevocably committed to issue the operative credit or amendment, without delay, in terms not inconsistent with the pre-advice.

Under review: Article 11

Equivalent article in UCP 500:

UCP 600, Article 11.a: UCP 500 articles 11.a.i and 11.a.ii

UCP 600 article 11.b: UCP 500 article 11.

Analysis:

UCP 600 article 11.a (first paragraph): UCP 500 article 11.a.i is greatly abbreviated and also simplified at the same time in UCP 600. The second half of the same article 11.a.i of UCP 500 had stated, 'Should a mail confirmation nevertheless be sent, it will have no effect and the Advising Bank will have no obligation to check such mail confirmation against the operative Credit instrument or the operative amendment received by teletransmission'. In the revised article of UCP 600, the essence of this sentence has been encompassed in a short, single phrase viz., 'shall be disregarded'.

UCP 600 article 11.a (second paragraph): Article 11.a.ii of UCP 500 has been reproduced almost exactly in UCP 600.

UCP 600 article 11.b: A subtle but significant change compared to that in UCP 500 has been introduced in the text of this article. A feature available in the earlier version provided the issuer of the pre-advice to retain an option of *not issuing the operative credit instrument or amendment*. A potentially dangerous provision, which could have been misused, has been deleted from the current text.

Comments: The most significant and the operative part of this article 11.c, the second sentence of this section in UCP 500, had begun with the words 'Unless otherwise stated in such preliminary advice by the Issuing Bank, an Issuing Bank having given such pre-advice shall be irrevocably...' etc. The words 'unless otherwise stated in such preliminary advice' had a very serious and dangerous implication in that the very purpose of the article would have been defeated. Issuing banks could have taken shelter under such exceptions, and could possibly have refrained from following up on its initial commitment. If not taken note of in the pre-advice, the beneficiary could face serious problems if it made any commitment or compromised its position based on such (revocable) pre-advices. That danger is now removed.

+++

ARTICLE 12: NOMINATION

a. Unless the nominated bank is the confirming bank, an authorisation to honour or negotiate does not impose any obligation on the nominated bank to honour or negotiate, except where expressly agreed to by the nominated bank and communicated to the beneficiary.

b. By nominating a bank to accept or incur a deferred payment undertaking, an issuing bank authorizes that nominated bank to prepay or purchase a draft accepted or a deferred payment undertaking incurred by that nominated bank.

c. Receipt or examination and forwarding of documents by a nominated bank that is not a confirming bank does not make that nominated bank liable to honour or negotiate, nor does it constitute honour or negotiation.

Under review: Article 12(a)

Equivalent article in UCP 500: Article 10.c

Analysis:

UCP 600 article 12(a): This is a redrafted and improved version of article 10(c) in UCP 500. The significance of the term 'honour' (effectively meaning 'to pay, incur a deferred payment undertaking, accept draft(s) against documents which appear on their face to be in compliance with the terms and conditions of the credit') used in conjunction with 'negotiation' in this article, is to be noted.

So far as a bank nominated by the issuing bank is concerned, the issue had always been about its obligations to the beneficiary (to honour or negotiate). The circumstances under which such obligations of a nominated bank arose had never been clearly stated in UCP 500.

This article (no. 12.a) now conveys very clearly that:

a. A confirming bank advises a credit *with engagement* (our favourite, antiquated, somewhat vague term), *i.e. with obligation* to the beneficiary, to honour or to negotiate a complying presentation.

b. A bank that is *not a confirming bank* advises a credit *without engagement, i.e.* without 'obligation' to the beneficiary, to honour or to negotiate if complying documents are presented under a credit. Mere advising does not constitute an obligation or undertaking to honour or to negotiate, *UNLESS*

c. The non-confirming bank, while advising the credit to the beneficiary, (i) *expressly agrees* to honour or negotiate, and simultaneously (ii) *communicates* that intention or willingness to the beneficiary. However, this remains a matter between the beneficiary and the concerned bank, and is outside the scope of the UCP. It's known as 'silent confirmation'.[89]

Comments: The whole issue about advising bank *expressly agreeing* has been emphasised in UCP 600 at two places. Article 9(a) states that an advising bank that is *not* a confirming bank advises a credit or an amendment *without obligation/undertaking* to honour or negotiate.

Article 12(a) extends the same logic a step further. It states that mere nomination or authorisation of a bank by the issuing bank to honour or negotiate does not impose any obligation on the bank so authorised or nominated to honour or negotiate, unless the bank so nominated has *expressly agreed* to that effect, and has accordingly advised the beneficiary. Further, the act of receipt, examination or the forwarding of documents by the nominated bank, if it is not a confirming bank, does not impose any obligation on that bank to honour or negotiate.

Article 8(b) states that a confirming bank is irrevocably bound to honour or negotiate. Article 12(a) above implies exactly the same position, provided certain conditions have been met.

In actual fact, the double-negatives and exceptions (through the use of phrases like 'unless stated otherwise',

---

[89] Refer to chapter 5, section 5.7.7 of the book *Beyond Trade Finance* by this author for more on 'silent confirmation'.

'except where expressly agreed' etc.) in UCP 500 article 10.c have now been done away with. The clauses were redrafted prior to their incorporation in UCP 600. The rules have been restated in simpler language. The articles, redrafted and rephrased, convey a positive directive at all times. The implications and purpose of the articles are now much easier to understand and appreciate.

Incidentally, article 12(a) imposes 'an (apparent) obligation on the nominated bank to honour or negotiate' but only where 'expressly agreed to by the nominated bank and communicated to the beneficiary'. Even this is a myth. This undertaking may be revoked if, say, risk parameters deteriorate. The obligation is not binding and is subject to the terms agreed privately between the bank and the beneficiary (see note on 'silent confirmation')

ARTICLE 12 (analysis contd....)

Under review: Article 12(b) and 12(c).

Equivalent article in UCP 500:

UCP 600 article 12.b: UCP 500 article 10.d

UCP 600 article 12.c: UCP 500 article 10.c (latter part)

Analysis:

Article 12.b: This article signifies a major change introduced through UCP 600. The UCP now recognises deferred payment undertaking, especially the discounting of drafts. The article offers protection to the nominated bank as holder in due course in case of fraud and if accepting bank gets its draft discounted.[90]

Reimbursement would be due on maturity whether or not draft or deferred payment undertaking is prepaid or purchased.

Comments:

Even though article 12(b) of UCP 600 allows a 'nominated bank to prepay or purchase a draft accepted or a deferred payment undertaking incurred by that nominated bank...' due caution should be exercised prior to making this move. This particular provision was introduced only in UCP 600 (consequent to the judgments in the Banco Santander case), and is yet to be tested in a court of law.

+++

---

[90] Refer to chapter 1, section 1.8.8 on deferred payment credits.

ARTICLE 13: BANK-TO-BANK REIMBURSEMENT ARRANGEMENTS

a. If a credit states that reimbursement is to be obtained by a nominated bank ('claiming bank') claiming on another party ('reimbursing bank'), the credit must state if the reimbursement is subject to the ICC rules for bank-to-bank reimbursements in effect on the date of issuance of the credit.

b. If a credit does not state that reimbursement is subject to the ICC rules for bank-to-bank reimbursements, the following apply:

   i. An issuing bank must provide a reimbursing bank with a reimbursement authorisation that conforms to the availability stated in the credit. The reimbursement authorisation should not be subject to an expiry date.

   ii. A claiming bank shall not be required to supply a reimbursing bank with a certificate of compliance with the terms and conditions of the credit.

   iii. An issuing bank will be responsible for any loss of interest, together with any expenses incurred, if reimbursement is not provided on first demand by the reimbursing bank in accordance with the terms and conditions of the credit.

   iv. A reimbursing bank's charges are for the account of the issuing bank. However, if the charges are for the account of the beneficiary, it is the responsibility of an issuing bank to so indicate in the credit and in the reimbursement authorisation. If a reimbursing bank's charges are for the account of the beneficiary, they shall be deducted from the amount due to the claiming bank when reimbursement is made. If no reimbursement is made, the reimbursing bank's charges remain the obligation of the issuing bank.

c. An issuing bank is not relieved from any of its obligations to provide reimbursement if reimbursement is not made by a reimbursing bank on first demand.

Under review: Article 13(a).

Equivalent article in UCP 500: New

Analysis:

This sub-section, the opening paragraph of article 13, lays down the ground rules for all bank-to-bank reimbursements. Article 13(a) stipulates that bank-to-bank reimbursement provisions in a documentary credit must be subjected to the relevant ICC rules for reimbursements applicable on the date of the issuance of the credit. By this stipulation, the ICC ensures continuing compliance with the prevalent ICC Uniform Rules for Bank-to-bank Reimbursement (URR), and protection thereunder to the parties concerned. Since separate rules on reimbursements exist[91], detailed procedural guidelines in the UCP are thereby avoided.

If a credit fails to subject itself to ICC Rules on bank-to-bank reimbursements, article 13(b) kicks in.

Comments: In the case of a credit subject to UCP 500, the reimbursement procedure is automatically subject to UCP 500. In UCP 600, it is *not* so.

On instances where no explicit reference to URR is made in the credit, however, the major part of article 13, viz., article 13.b reinforces virtually the same procedures as laid down in the URR.

ARTICLE 13 (analysis contd....)

Under review: Article 13(b) and 13(c).

Equivalent article in UCP 500:

- UCP 600 article 13.b.i: UCP 500 article 19.a
- UCP 600 article 13.b.ii: UCP 500 article 19.b
- UCP 600 article 13.b.iii: UCP 500 article 19.d
- UCP 600 article 13.b.iv: UCP 500 article 19.e
- UCP 600 article 13.c: UCP 500 article 19.c

---

[91] As on the date of UCP 600 coming into operation, the applicable URR was ICC Publication No. 525, replaced by ICC Publication No. 725 (URR 725) with effect from 1 October 2008.

Analysis:

UCP 600 article 13.b.i: The words '...with proper instructions or authorisation to honour...' in article 19(a) of UCP 500 has been replaced with '...reimbursement authorisation that conforms to the availability stated in the credit'. (The words 'proper instructions' convey nothing specific in terms of rules for compliance; such 'rules' cannot be enforced, hence better avoided.)

Reimbursement authorisation subject to article 13(b) must not include an expiry date. The reference to 'expiry date', though new to the UCP, is in line with URR which contains this provision.

UCP 600 article 13.b.ii: No change.

UCP 600 article 13.b.iii: No change.

UCP 600 article 13.b.iv: It stipulates that reimbursing bank's charges are for the account of the issuing bank. If they are to be paid by the beneficiary (instead of 'another party' as stated in article 19(e) of UCP 500) it must be indicated accordingly in the credit and in the reimbursement authorisation.

A change in procedure in UCP 600 from that in UCP 500 is that, if a reimbursing bank's charges are payable by ('for the account of') the beneficiary, the reimbursing bank is now being permitted to *deduct* its charges from the amount paid to the claiming bank (with obvious benefits). In UCP 500, the reimbursing bank had to *collect* its charges from the claiming bank.

UCP 600 article 13(c): The clause 'if and when reimbursement is not received by the Claiming Bank…' has been replaced with 'if reimbursement is not made by a reimbursing bank on first demand'. The modification shifts the onus to the reimbursing bank, makes the process transparent and the performance specific (the trigger being '*on first demand*').

Comments:

Through subtle but significant changes in the drafting of article 13(a) and 13(b), a larger role of URR in all future bank-to-bank reimbursements has been provided for.

+++

ARTICLE 14: STANDARD FOR EXAMINATION OF DOCUMENTS

a. A nominated bank acting on its nomination, a confirming bank, if any, and the issuing bank must examine a presentation to determine, on the basis of the documents alone, whether or not the documents appear on their face to constitute a complying presentation.

b. A nominated bank acting on its nomination, a confirming bank, if any, and the issuing bank shall each have a maximum of five banking days following the day of presentation to determine if a presentation is complying. This period is not curtailed or otherwise affected by the occurrence on or after the date of presentation of any expiry date or last day for presentation.

c. A presentation including one or more original transport documents subject to articles 19, 20, 21, 22, 23, 24 or 25 must be made by or on behalf of the beneficiary not later than 21 calendar days after the date of shipment as described in these rules, but in any event not later than the expiry date of the credit.

d. Data in a document, when read in context with the credit, the document itself and international standard banking practice, need not be identical to, but must not conflict with, data in that document, any other stipulated document or the credit.

e. In documents other than commercial invoice, the description of the goods, services or performance, if stated, may be in general terms not conflicting with their description in the credit.

f. If a credit requires presentation of a document other than a transport document, insurance document or commercial invoice, without stipulating by whom the document is to be issued or its data content, banks will accept the document as presented if its content appears to fulfil the function of the required document and otherwise complies with article 14(d).

g. A document presented but not required by the credit will be disregarded and may be returned to the presenter.

h. If a credit contains a condition without stipulating the document to indicate compliance with the condition, banks will deem such condition as not stated and will disregard it.

i. A document may be dated prior to the issuance date of the credit, but must not be dated later than its date of presentation.

j. When the addresses of the beneficiary and the applicant appear in any stipulated document, they need not be the same as those stated in the credit or in any other stipulated document, but must be within the same country as the respective addresses mentioned in the credit. Contact details (telefax, telephone, email and the like) stated as part of the beneficiary's and the applicant's address will be disregarded. However, when the address and the contact details of the applicant appear as part of the consignee or notify party details on a transport document subject to articles 19, 20, 21, 22, 23, 24 or 25, they must be as stated in the credit.

k. The shipper/consignor of the goods indicated on any document need not be the beneficiary of the credit.

l. A transport document may be issued by any party other than a carrier, owner, master or charterer provided that the transport document meets the requirements of articles 19, 20, 21, 22, 23, or 24 of these rules.

Under review: Article 14.a

Equivalent article in UCP 500: Article 13.a

Analysis:

Significant change has been effected in identifying the examining banks. Article 13(a) (Standard for Examination of Documents) in UCP 500 began with the words 'Banks must examine...'. The fact is that, under the provisions of the UCP, *not every bank* needs to examine (documents). In UCP 500, this position had also been clearly reiterated at the beginning of article 14(b) itself, but not in article 13(a).

Therefore, in this article, the banks charged with the responsibilities envisaged were required to be defined. The modification now clarifies who will examine (the documents). For example, only if a nominated bank is willing to act on its nomination, will examine; if it is not willing to act on its nomination, there is no need for it to examine (the documents).

Comments:

The definition 'complying presentation' replaces the clause in article 13.a of UCP 500 ('Compliances of the stipulated documents... in these articles') conveying the same meaning.

The critically important and one of the most important of all clauses in documentary credit operations '...must determine on the basis of documents alone whether....' appears in article 14(b) of UCP 500. This clause has been merged with article 14(a) in UCP 600. The structure of this article (article 13(a) in UCP 500) has, at the same time, been considerably simplified and improved.

A significant point to note is that this is the *only* place in the whole of UCP 600 where reference to the contentious phrase 'on its face' from UCP 500 article 14(b) has been retained. Section 1.8.3 provides further information on this subject and detailed background to this important and hotly debated issue.

Together with article 4 and article 5, this sub-article in essence establishes the independence principle of a documentary credit. This means that a bank's obligation under an LC is determined only by the terms of the credit and a complying presentation.

Under review: Article 14.b

Equivalent article in UCP 500: Article 13.b

Analysis:

Maximum period for examination of documents and for informing the presenter *reduced* from seven banking days to five banking days.

The expression 'reasonable time' has been deleted from the earlier article 13(b) in UCP 500.

Comments:

None.

ARTICLE 14 (analysis contd....)

Under review: Article 14(c)

Equivalent article in UCP 500: Article 43.a.

Analysis:

Default period of 21 days for presentation applies only where an original transport document is included in the presentation. (Different rules come into play when a presentation includes only copies of transport documents, no original. Refer to chapter 10 section 1.8 of the book *Letters of credit: Theory and practice* by this author for details.)

The requirement in UCP 500 article 43(a) that 'every credit...should also stipulate a specified period of time after the date of shipment during which presentation must be made...' was deleted from article 14(c) of UCP 600.

The relevant article in UCP 500 was restructured and simplified in UCP 600.

Comments:

The period of 21 days is the 'default option', the *maximum* period allowed within the validity of the credit. Yet, from a practical point of view, it is necessary that 'every credit must stipulate a specified period of time after the date of shipment during which presentation must be made'. This is because for every shipment a considered view should be taken by the importer and the issuing bank, on a case-by-case basis, how quickly the documents must be released by the beneficiary.

For example, when goods are transported by air, or consignments are scheduled to cover short distances between despatch and delivery points, the default option of 21 days could be against the best interest of the buyer. It is felt that retention of the stipulation ('every credit…must be made'), though somewhat advisory in nature, in the revised version of the UCP would have been helpful in this context.

ARTICLE 14 (analysis contd……)

Under review: Article 14(d)

Equivalent article in UCP 500: Article 13.a.

Analysis:

In this article 14(d) the 'inconsistency' rule from UCP 500 was replaced by a 'not in conflict' rule. The new phrases ' … in context with…' and '… need not be identical to…' introduce a conscious shift away from the *mirror image* style for examination of documents advocated till UCP 500. In addition it is now stressed that the data must be read in context. The current indication is to move away from a copy-cat approach to a more mature application of mind. ISBP 745 articles L5 and L6 are very good examples of this approach.

The phrase 'international standard banking practice as reflected in these articles' in UCP 500 was modified. The words 'as reflected in these articles' were deleted. The expression 'International standard banking practice' is used in this article as a general expression with wider significance and application, its meaning not necessarily being restricted to the ICC Publication[92] alone (hence the initials have not been capitalised).

Comments:

Divergent opinion was expressed within the Drafting Group regarding specific reference to the ISBP in the UCP, removal of all reference to international standard banking practice, and whether a reference to the ISBP detracted from the essence of the UCP. As explained earlier, the expression 'international standard banking practice' is being used here in a broader sense.[93]

The word 'context' ('when read in context...') is significant, since certain descriptions are now permitted to be stated 'in general terms *not conflicting* with their description in the credit' (see next article). Further, in order to be compliant, the content or the *purpose* of a document presented must agree in general terms with the stated

---

[92] International Standard Banking Practice (ISBP), ICC Publication No. 645, or No. 681 (as on the date of implementation of UCP 600) or the version currently operative (ISBP 745).

[93] Refer to chapter 1 section 1.8.6 for more on this issue.

purpose of the credit.[94] In other words, the emphasis is on contextual relationship, not mirror identity.

One may observe that the section appearing after the words '... must not conflict with' is a conscious attempt to redefine and replace the clause 'documents which appear *on their face to be inconsistent with one another...'* (Clause in article 13.a, UCP 500 – subject of debate in Drafting Group). Refer to chapter 2, section 2.6.12 for more information on this subject.

The modification reflects a similar provision in the currently operative ISBP ICC Publication No. 745.[95].

----

[94] Article 41 of ISBP 681 stipulates that documents may bear a title as required by the credit, have a title similar to that stipulated in the credit or be untitled; but its contents must appear to fulfil the function of the required document. Refer also to ICC ISBP 745 article A39 on the same issue.

[95] The issue of 'inconsistency' is modified in ISBP, ICC Publication No. 745. The concerned article that was present in ISBP 645 was deleted from ISBP 681. It's now about conflict of data. Also refer to chapter 2, section 2.8.4 regarding title of documents.

ARTICLE 14 (analysis contd....)

Under review: Article 14.e

Equivalent article in UCP 500: Article 37.c (second and last sentence).

Analysis:

This section in article 37.c of UCP 500 which states 'In all other documents, the goods may be described in general terms not inconsistent with the description of the goods in the Credit', was detached from the first part relating to 'commercial invoice' and placed separately as an independent article.

Note that there is no requirement that documents other than the invoice indicate the description of goods. This even applies to the bill of lading (refer to Official ICC Opinion TA.681rev, March 2009).

Comments:

Stipulations with regard to the contents of and descriptions of goods in an invoice have been covered in the UCP and more elaborately in the ISBP[96]. Greater purpose has been served by expanding the coverage of the provisions of this article and making it applicable to other documents.

---

[96] ISBP 745 sections C.3 to C.14.

ARTICLE 14 (analysis contd....)

Under review:

Article 14.f

Article 14.g

Article 14.h

Equivalent article in UCP 500:

UCP 600 article 14.f: UCP 500 article 21

UCP 600 article 14.g: UCP 500 article 13.a (second part)

UCP 600 article 14.h: UCP 500 article 13.c

Analysis:

UCP 600 article 14.f: In UCP 500 the first word 'when' in article 21 titled 'Unspecified Issuers or Contents of Documents' was replaced in this article of UCP 600 with the word 'if'.

The clause in UCP 500 article 21 that stated '... provided their data content is not inconsistent with any other stipulated document presented' was replaced with 'if it's content appears to fulfil the function of the required document'.

The second change is significant. Henceforth, submission of *any* document (except a transport document, insurance document and commercial invoice) with *any* title that apparently meets with the terms of the credit would not suffice. The contents of the document must *appear to fulfil the function of the required document* – irrespective of what the title says, or even if the title is absent.[97]

It also continued with the concept that where a credit did not indicate who must issue a document (other than the aforementioned), it could be issued by anyone.

UCP 600 article 14.g: No change in meaning. In the second paragraph in article 13.a of UCP 500 the stipulation '.... shall return them to the presenter or pass them on without responsibility' was modified by deleting the words 'pass them on without responsibility'. The word 'shall' was replaced with 'may', as the former term was a misfit here ('shall' makes an instruction mandatory, it should not be followed by an option).

UCP 600 article 14.h: No change.

Comments:

UCP 500 article 13.c (on 'non-documentary conditions', stating that if a credit stipulated conditions without relating them to documents that should be produced in compliance of such conditions ....etc.): An element of confusion and misinterpretation of this clause in the UCP was introduced by Position Paper No. 3 of The ICC Banking Commission. In effect it stated that a so-called 'non-documentary' condition may be found to have actually been complied with through suitable textual

---

[97] An instance of content being given precedence over container, so to say.

evidence in another document within the set presented. The relevant paragraph was as follows:

> 'Sometimes, however, a condition appears in a documentary credit which can be clearly linked to a document stipulated in that documentary credit. Such a condition is not then deemed to be a non-documentary condition. For example, if a condition in the documentary credit states that the goods are to be of German origin and no Certificate of Origin is called for, the reference to 'German origin' would be deemed to be a non-documentary condition and disregarded in accordance with UCP 500 article 13(c). If, however, the same documentary credit stipulated a Certificate of Origin, then there would not be a non-documentary condition as the Certificate of Origin would have to evidence the German origin. (See also ICC Publication No. 511, 'UCP 500 and 400 Compared, page 42.)'

This position went against the spirit of the UCP. It also introduced an element of subjectivity, created room for confusion and consequently became a debatable issue. The point of view expressed in this Position Paper demanded clarification.

UCP 600 supersedes this Position Paper (as also it supersedes all previously issued Position Papers; they are valid no longer since UCP 600 was introduced). The issue is now clear and the UCP is without any ambiguity.

UCP 500 article 13(a) included another provision without providing clarification. This was with regard to the responsibilities of an issuing bank if and when it received a document forwarded to it but which was not called for in the credit. The UCP did not state what the issuing bank was supposed to do with it. Such an action by the nominated bank, though confusing and undesirable, would clearly have been within the provisions of (and hence approved by) the UCP but confusing for the issuing bank.[98] The modification in the article in UCP 600 has done away with the problem provision.

ARTICLE 14 (analysis contd....)

Under review:

Article 14.i [99]

Article 14.j

Article 14.k

Article 14.l

Equivalent article in UCP 500:

- UCP 600 article 14.j: UCP 500 article 22
- UCP 600 article 14.j: New

---

[98] Refer to chapter 2, sections 2.6.10 and 2.6.11.

[99] Also refer to articles 13 and 14, ISBP (ICC Publication No. 681), or ISBP 745 articles A.11 to A.16.

- UCP 600 article 14.k: UCP 500 article 31.iii
- UCP 600 article 14.l: UCP 500 article 30

Analysis:

UCP 600 article 14.i: Structure slightly modified. No change in meaning. This sub-article represents a common-sense approach to dates of documents. It states that banks generally cannot accept documents bearing a future date from the date on which it is presented, but (unless the LC states otherwise) banks may accept documents dated before the date of issue of an LC.

UCP 600 article 14.j: It's new, but in tune with the provisions in the ISBP. Variations in addresses were considered a discrepancy till ISBP ICC Publication No. 645 was issued, which stipulated otherwise. Since this provision was introduced in UCP 600, a reference to it was removed from the next version of ISBP, ICC Publication No. 681, which came into effect from the same date as did UCP 600, i.e., on 1 July 2007. ISBP 745 continues with the same provision.

Changes in the opening line made to reflect the address of applicant that may be required to appear on a specific document (viz., a transport document). Though this article accepts the possibility that addresses of the applicant and of the beneficiary in some documents could be different from that stated in a credit, it is obvious that the contact details of the applicant (as the consignee) or the party to be notified (on arrival of goods) should not differ from that required in the credit. Else the system will not work. The provisions are self-explicit.

Since the article is new there is no documented practice yet, and especially when it comes to the stated exception, there is a need to exercise caution in its application.

UCP 600 article 14.k: Article 31.iii of UCP 500 referred only to transport documents. The scope of this article was widened to provide for the fact that the shipper or the consignor – as marked not only in a transport document, but in *any* document – need not be the beneficiary of the credit. The requirement of transferable credits is thus accommodated.

UCP 600 article 14.l: The much discussed and debated issue regarding retention or otherwise of article 30, UCP 500 (transport documents issued by freight forwarders) was taken care of through this article. This article is an attempt to modernize UCP 500 article 30 in a way so that it is not limited to freight forwarders but rather to any issuer of transport documents presented under an LC.

Comments:

UCP 600 article 14.i: Assuming that the date on a document is the date of its preparation or creation, it should be obvious that a document ought not to bear a date that is later than its date of presentation. Though this provision was not in UCP 500, it was introduced UCP 600.

UCP 600 article 14.j: The rationale for this clause is that a beneficiary may have offices at separate locations for specific purposes (e.g. finance department in one city – dealing with banking and LCs, import department in another city - handling shipment inward, necessitating multiple addresses for the same credit). Some of the concerns that were expressed on this change by members of the Drafting Group were on the following lines:

a. Did it really matter if addresses that were not the same were in the same country or not?

b. In some countries different companies share the same name. If their respective addresses were not used for identification, how would one know whether Company X was different from Company Y?

c. The new language used in the UCP meant that in all documents, the address of the beneficiary or the address of the applicant did not matter at all.

d. The new provision could lead to instances of fraud.

The words used in this article, while retaining the spirit of the ISBP, take care of these concerns to a considerable extent.

UCP 600 article 14.l: Article 30 of UCP 500 was not deemed to be necessary as UCP does not define who has to 'issue' the transport document. It was pointed out that this sub-section permitted a transport document to be issued by any party other than a carrier, owner, master or charter; which meant that a freight forwarder was also included in this general permission provided the document conformed to the applicable article of the UCP[100]. Yet, the transport lobby was extremely concerned about the proposal to remove article 30 from the new version of the UCP.

+++

[100] Refer to chapter 1, section 1.8.10 for further details.

ARTICLE 15: COMPLYING PRESENTATION

a. When an issuing bank determines that a presentation is complying, it must honour.

b. When a confirming bank determines that a presentation is complying, it must honour or negotiate and forward the documents to the issuing bank.

c. When a nominated bank determines that a presentation is complying and honours or negotiates, it must forward the documents to the confirming bank or issuing bank.

Under review:

Articles 15.a,, 15.b, 15.c

Equivalent article in UCP 500: Article 9.

Analysis:

Duties of the nominated bank, the confirming bank and the issuing bank subsequent to the presentation of documents under a credit are stated in clear terms.

Article 9 of UCP 500 laid down the 'definite undertaking' of these banks 'if' the credit provided for either sight payment, acceptance, deferred payment or negotiation. The 'if' in the construction of the respective articles has been replaced by 'when', to emphasize the next course of action after a presentation has been found to be *complying*.

This revised and redrafted article outlines the principle that when a complying presentation to the issuing or the confirming banks has been made, these banks must honour or negotiate the documents. The article follows this directive by stating that, in addition, the complying documents must be forwarded to the confirming or the issuing bank, as applicable.

When is that 'when', is not defined. It could be weeks, months or more. This lack of any clear time limit, or even a moral suasion (like 'without delay'), opens the door to various problems for the issuing bank. Because, under article 7(a) it continues to be bound by its own commitment to honour a presentation – for how long, not stated – irrespective of how long the nominated bank may take to despatch the shipping documents. For more on this problem issue, refer to chapter 11 section 11.13 of the book *Letters of credit: Theory and practice* by this author.

Comments:

UCP 500 had spelt out the steps to be followed when documents were found to be not as per the term of the credit, i.e. 'discrepant'. But nowhere in UCP 500 had it been stated (except by implication) *when,* or under what circumstances, a bank became duty-bound to honour or to negotiate. As far as an issuing bank or a confirming bank was concerned, articles 15(a) and 15(b) did well to establish the position clearly.

That left us with sub-section UCP 600 article 15(c). We do recognise the fact that a nominated bank has certain obligations and privileges under articles 12(a) and 12(c). A nominated bank that advises *without obligation*, gives no undertaking to honour or to negotiate (article 9.a UCP 600). The problem for the beneficiary would arise where a nominated bank determined that a presentation *was* complying but still refused to honour or negotiate. Or, what if it considerably delayed forwarding the documents after negotiation? No UCP rule required a nominated bank to comply with either of these or provided a remedy for the affected parties.

The beneficiary may have no option but to seek relief with the issuing bank under article 7, *provided it had at its disposal sufficient time to ensure that the documents reached the issuing bank before the credit expired.* As stated earlier, the issuing bank could suffer too, as described in chapter 11, section 11.13 of the book *Letters of credit: Theory and practice* by this author. Article 15 still remains a very weak provision in UCP 600.

+++

ARTICLE 16: DISCREPANT DOCUMENTS, WAIVER AND NOTICE

a. When a nominated bank acting on its nomination, a confirming bank, if any, or the issuing bank determines that a presentation does not comply, it may refuse to honour or negotiate.

b. When an issuing bank determines that a presentation does not comply, it may in its sole judgement approach the applicant for a waiver of the discrepancies. This does not, however, extend the period mentioned in article 14(b).

c. When a nominated bank acting on its nomination, a confirming bank, if any, or the issuing bank decides to refuse to honour or negotiate, it must give a single notice to that effect to the presenter.

The notice must state:

i. that the bank is refusing to honour or negotiate; and

ii. each discrepancy in respect of which the bank refuses to honour or negotiate; and

iii. (a) that the bank is holding the documents pending further instructions from the presenter; or

(b) that the issuing bank is holding the documents until it receives a waiver from the applicant and agrees to accept it, or receives further instructions from the presenter prior to agreeing to accept a waiver; or

(c) that the bank is returning the documents; or

(d) that the bank is acting in accordance with instructions previously received from the presenter.

d. The notice required in article 16(c) must be given by telecommunication or, if that is not possible, by other expeditious means no later than the close of the fifth banking day following the day of presentation.

e. A nominated bank acting on its nomination, a confirming bank, if any, or the issuing bank may, after providing notice required by the article 16(c) (iii) (a) or (b), return the documents to the presenter at any time.

f. If an issuing bank or a confirming bank fails to act in accordance with the provisions of this article, it shall be precluded from claiming that the documents do not constitute a complying presentation.

g. When an issuing bank refuses to honour or a confirming bank refuses to honour or negotiate and has given notice to that effect in accordance with this article, it shall then be entitled to claim a refund, with interest, of any reimbursement made.

Under review: Articles 16(a) and 16(b)

Equivalent article in UCP 500:

UCP 600 article 16.a: UCP 500 article 14.b.

UCP 600 article 16.b: UCP 500 article 14.c

Analysis:

UCP 600 article 16.a: Not all banks are required to examine documents to confirm a complying presentation[101]. For this reason the applicable banks have, once again, been defined.

The much-debated expression 'on their face'[102] – in article 14.b of UCP 500 – was deleted from the revised version of this article (as also from almost all places in UCP 600).

The phrase 'take up the documents' in UCP 500 article 14.b in the section '... such banks may refuse to take up the documents' was in frequent use over several decades. But there was always a possibility that the expression may not always convey in exact terms the desired intention (negotiate or honour) that it was meant to convey. The term could also be subject to misinterpretation or wrong translation. The relevant section of the article was, therefore, redrafted to read as 'may refuse to honour or negotiate'.

---

[101] Refer to chapter 2, sections 2.2.1., 2.2.2, 2.6.12, and 2.7 for more on discrepant documents.

[102] Refer to chapter 1, section 1.8.3.

The matter relating to 'must determine on the basis of documents alone' was moved to article 14.a in UCP 600. Apart from this, there is no change in meaning or in application from the article in UCP 500.

UCP 600 article 16.b: The expression 'on its face' deleted from text of UCP 500. The article, otherwise, remains unchanged in essence and meaning.

Comments:

This article gave rise to the maximum number of enquiries, and the maximum number of opinions by the ICC Banking Commission. Details are available in chapter 2, sections 2.2.1., 2.2.2, 2.6.5, and 2.7.

UCP 600 article 16.a: Apparently, the expression 'take up documents' could give rise to confusion similar to those that was created by the term 'on its face'. This section of the UCP, therefore, was modified and made more specific in its meaning and intent.

+++

ARTICLE 16: DISCREPANT DOCUMENTS, WAIVER AND NOTICE (analysis contd....)

Under review: Article 16(c)

Equivalent article in UCP 500:

Articles 14.d.i and 14.d.ii

Analysis:

Article 16.c: The section of this article in UCP 600 finds an echo in UCP 500, articles 14(d)(i) and d(ii). However, the sentences have been rearranged so that subjects with the same reference appear together at one place. Further, the rules now appear in a logical sequence. (This was not so in UCP 500.)

Accordingly, in this article of UCP 600, first comes the decision to refuse, next is the matter of notice to the presenter about the refusal. The expression 'single notice' in article 14.c (UCP 600) seeks to replace 'Such notice must state all discrepancies (in respect of which the bank refuses ...' etc.) in article 14(d)(ii) of UCP 500. This could have been retained in UCP 600, since the words 'single notice' do not emphatically convey the message that *all discrepancies* must be stated the very first time and only once, that the bank cannot come back later to advise additional discrepancies. This fact has to be concluded from the two expressions that must be read together with article 16(c)(ii) that follows. [103]

Review of articles 16(c)(i) to 16(c)(iii): Refusal notice has three distinctive steps.

a. The first is the message that the bank is refusing to honour or negotiate.

b. The second is the communication of each and every discrepancy leading to the refusal.

c. The third is the status of the handling of the documents, being one of the four options in UCP 600 under article 16, article c.iii(a), c.iii(b), c.iii(c) or c.iii(d).

The four options provided in UCP 600 are:

i. holding of documents further instructions from the presenter,

ii. holding the documents until the bank receives a waiver and agrees to accept it or receives further

---

[103] This author is not comfortable with the revised draft, and believes that the words 'single notice' does not effectively convey the requirement that the notice must be the first, the last and the only one; that it should contain all discrepancies at one go; and that the scrutinising bank does not have the privilege of coming up with more discrepancies at a later date, *after* the first notice had been sent. The term 'single notice' - even if read in conjunction with 'each discrepancy' in article 16(c)(ii) of UCP 600 - does not effectively add up to the same meaning as 'all discrepancies' in article 14(d)(ii) of UCP 500.

instructions from the presenter prior to agreeing to accept a waiver104,

iii. returning documents, and

iv. bank acting in accordance with instructions previously received from the presenter.

Comments:

If the notice of refusal is made by means of SWIFT using message type MT734 it is understood that the banks is refusing the presentation.

In making a routine waiver request, the issuing bank should make it clear that its request for waiver represents no commitment or obligation of the issuing bank to waive discrepancies should the applicant decide to waive discrepancies.

> "It must be remembered that if discrepant documents are presented, that presentation, in effect, amounts to a request to modify the LC. No modification is effective legally without consent of all parties, that is, issuer, beneficiary, and applicant. To consent to a modification request requires an intentional act.

---

[104] This goes against the accepted principle that discrepant documents belong to the beneficiary. Even if applicant accepts discrepancies, final delivery or disposal of the documents by the issuing bank ought to be in accordance with prior approval of or in accordance with instructions from the beneficiary. A reading of the article in its present form fails to make that position clear.

An issuer has no obligation to agree to a modification of its LC (i.e., agree to pay against discrepant documents) even if the applicant is willing that it do so. Therefore, the applicant's willingness to waive discrepancies should not, in itself, bind the issuer to pay." *Robert M. Rosenblith, Esq.*

ARTICLE 16: DISCREPANT DOCUMENTS, WAIVER AND NOTICE (analysis contd....)

Under review:

Articles 16(d), 16(e), 16(f) and 16(g)

Equivalent article in UCP 500:

UCP 600 article 16.d: UCP 500 article 14.d.i (part)

UCP 600 article 16.e: No direct equivalent in UCP 500

UCP 600 article 16.f: UCP 500 article 14.e

UCP 600 article 16.g: UCP 500 article 14.e

Analysis:

UCP 600 article 16.d: The article reflects the maximum period of five banking days referred to under article 14(b) titled 'Standard for Examination of Documents'. The period stands reduced from seven banking days that was available under UCP 500.

The expression 'without delay', present in article 14.d.i, UCP 500, stands deleted in the revised text of article 16(d) (UCP 600).

UCP 600 article 16(e): Applicable banks are uniformly defined. A more positive, direct sentence replaces a negative structure in UCP 500 article 14. This article states clearly at which point a scrutinising bank is free to return the documents without further reference.

This clarity in direction was not available in UCP 500 (no equivalent article). 'Returning to presenter' had been mentioned in article 13(d)(ii) as one of the options concurrent with the serving of notice of refusal. The stage at which '... return to presenter....' came into play is marginally altered here. This article clarifies that if a bank *has* provided a notice of refusal *and* chosen option (a) or (b) (of article 16.c.iii), it may return the documents at any time thereafter.[105]

UCP 600 article 16.f: No change.

UCP 600 article 16.g: No change.

Comments: The arrangement of the articles maintains a logical and natural sequence of events/steps.

Article 16.d: The relevant section of article 14(d)(i) of UCP 500 had stipulated as follows: '...must give notice to that

---

[105] This article is in line with clarification issued by the ICC vide ICC Banking Commission Recommendation Ref. Document 470/952rev2 on handling of Discrepant Documents.

effect by telecommunication or, if that is not possible, by other expeditious means, without delay but no later than the close of the seventh banking day…' etc. Though the period has been reduced to five banking days, the deletion of the expression 'without delay' removes the element of persuasion contained in the UCP, or the obligation of the bank concerned, to act as expeditiously as possible under a given circumstances.[106]

The word 'expeditious' has been used in relation to the means or the mode to be used for communication. But the bank concerned has been left to its own devices, and would have performed according to the UCP rules or under its own obligation if it acted no later than the close of the fifth banking day following the day of presentation. Note that, in this article, nothing otherwise has been expected nor asked for. Not a welcome step, in the opinion of this author.

UCP 500 article 14(f) completely omitted in UCP 600. The contents of this article have not been carried over to UCP 600 in any form. The provision was construed as a matter between a beneficiary and the nominated bank and therefore, irrelevant as far as the rules of the UCP were concerned. A confirming or issuing bank would anyway continue to take a view on the documents based on the provisions of Articles 14 and 16.

---

[106] Refer to chapter 2, section 2.5.5 for comments on this subject.

ARTICLE 17: ORIGINAL DOCUMENTS AND COPIES

a. At least one original of each document stipulated in the credit must be presented.

b. A bank shall treat as an original any document bearing an apparently original signature, mark, stamp, or label of the issuer of the document, unless the document itself indicates that it is not an original.

c. Unless a document indicates otherwise, a bank will also accept a document as original if it:

   i. appears to be written, typed, perforated or stamped by the document issuer's hand; or

   ii. appears to be on the document issuer's original stationery; or

   iii. states that it is original, unless the statement appears not to apply to the document presented.

d. If a credit requires presentation of copies of documents, presentation of either originals or copies is permitted.

e. If a credit requires presentation of multiple documents by using terms such as 'in duplicate', 'in two fold' or 'in two copies', this will be satisfied by the presentation of at least one original and the remaining number in copies, except when the document itself indicates otherwise.

Under review: Article 17

Equivalent article in UCP 500:

UCP 600 article 17.a: New

UCP 600 article 17.b: UCP 500 article 20.e

UCP 600 article 17.c: UCP 500 article 20.b

UCP 600 article 17.d: UCP 500 article 20.c.i

UCP 600 article 17.e: UCP 500 article 20.c.ii

Analysis:

UCP 600 article 17.a: This article is new. A passing mention had been made in article 20.c.ii (UCP 500) about presentation of one original ('Credits that require multiple document(s) such as 'duplicate', 'twofold', 'two copies' and the like, will be satisfied by the representation of one original and the remaining number in copies...'). But nowhere in UCP 500 had it been categorically stipulated that, unless only *copies* have been asked for, presentation of *at least one original* was a must. This revision makes it clear that – unless the credit stipulates otherwise – at least *one* of each set of documents must be an original.

UCP 600 article 17.b: The requirement of an original is based on concept in ICC Decision of Original Documents.[107]

---

[107] *The Determination of an 'Original' Document in the Context of UCP 500 article 20(b),* Document no 470/871, Rev. 29 July

UCP 600 article 17.c: Redrafted; no major change.

UCP 600 article 17 d: Words slightly modified and simplified.

UCP 600 article 17 e: No major change. This sub-section simply clarifies and reiterates the earlier position that where a credit calls for presentation of multiple documents, 'at least one original' is what is required to be presented.

Comments:

Although article 17 of UCP 600 is a revised version of article 20 in UCP 500, a few drafting changes have been effected. The first sub-section (article 20.a) was about terms such as 'first class', 'well known'. These were totally misplaced in this article that actually related to a description of original documents and copies. This section, i.e. article 14(a) of UCP 500, therefore, was segregated and moved under UCP 600 article 2 ('Definitions') with good reason.

The text was revised and rearranged.[108]

1999, ICC Commission on Banking Technique and Practice. Replaced by the presently operative provisions in the UCP and the ISBP.

[108] Though attempt was made to indicate the cross-references between the new text and the older version in UCP 500, it was on a best-effort basis as exact co-relation could not be established for reasons explained in the preface and elsewhere in this book.

Article 17.a (calling for at least one original) is an extension of article 32 of ISBP, ICC 645 ('Each required document must be presented in at least one original, unless the credit allows for presentation of documents as copies.'). [109]

Article 20(d) in UCP 500 was retained in UCP 600; but appropriately included under article 3 titled 'Interpretations'.

+++

---

[109] In its revised version of the ISBP (ICC 681), the article was modified and re-drafted to take into account the requirement of 'at least one original' referenced in article 17(a) of UCP 600. Refer to the currently applicable rules in ISBP 745 sections A.27 to A.31 which deals with originals and copies of documents.

ARTICLE 18: COMMERCIAL INVOICE

a. A commercial invoice:

   i. must appear to have been issued by the beneficiary (except as provided in article 38);

   ii. must be made out in the name of the applicant (except as provided in article 38 (g));

   iii. must be made out in the same currency as the credit; and

   iv. need not be signed.

b. A nominated bank acting on its nomination, a confirming bank, if any, or the issuing bank may accept a commercial invoice issued for an amount in excess of the amount permitted by the credit, and its decision will be binding upon all parties, provided the bank in question has not honoured or negotiated for an amount in excess of that permitted by the credit.

c. The description of the goods, services or performance in a commercial invoice must correspond with that which appears in the credit.

Under review:

Article 18

Equivalent article in UCP 500:

UCP 600 article 18.a: UCP 500 article 37.a.i to iii.

UCP 600 article 18.b: UCP 500 article 37.b

UCP 600 article 18.c: UCP 500 article 37.c

Analysis:

UCP 600 article 18.a: No change. Definitions of the term 'beneficiary', 'applicant' are as per article 1 of UCP 600. The only addition is article 18.a (iii) about the invoice being 'in the same currency as the credit'.

It has not been explained why a commercial invoice, one of the most important documents for the purposes of export or import clearance and other obligatory requirements, "need not be signed". A commercial invoice not requiring a signature is more often an exception than a rule. Because of this, nearly all credits require "*signed* commercial invoice", a chore that could have been avoided.

UCP 600 article 18.b: To prevent such eventualities as outlined in this article, the suggested remedy is to stipulate in the credit that the invoice value is not to exceed the credit amount. In the alternate, the LC condition may stipulate that documents (invoice) may be drawn up for a maximum amount of ..... (LC amount), or similar terms.

Emphasis in this article has been changed to the effect that banks *may* accept an invoice for a greater value, provided it does not honour or negotiate for an amount in excess of the credit.

UCP 600 article 18.c: No change from what had been stated in UCP 500, except the fact that 'services or performance' have been added.

Comments:

As such there is no requirement (in UCP 600) for the addresses or country of the beneficiary and applicant to be mentioned in the invoice. There may, however, be other reasons – for example, AML – for including such information. In that case UCP 600 sub-article 14(j) will apply.

The addition of article 18.a(iii) stipulating that a commercial invoice must be in the same currency as that of the credit may appear superfluous to us, since any deviation would anyway be *against* the terms and conditions of the credit and hence not acceptable.

In addition to the rules on commercial invoices stated in the UCP, ISBP 745 articles C3 to C14 (both inclusive) titled *Description of the goods, services or performance and other general issues related to invoices* provide critically important information with regard to commercial invoices presented under documentary credits.

+++

ARTICLE 19: TRANSPORT DOCUMENT COVERING AT LEAST TWO DIFFERENT MODES OF TRANSPORT

a. A transport document covering at least two different modes of transport (multimodal or combined transport document), however named, must appear to:

   i. indicate the name of the carrier and be signed by:

      - the carrier or a named agent for or on behalf of the carrier, or

      - the master or a named agent for or on behalf of the master.

      Any signature by the carrier, master or agent must be identified as that of the carrier, master or agent.

      Any signature by an agent must indicate whether the agent has signed for or on behalf of the carrier or for or on behalf of the master.

   ii. indicate that the goods have been dispatched, taken in charge or shipped on board at the place stated in the credit by:

      - pre-printed wording, or

      - a stamp or notation indicating the date on which the goods have been dispatched, taken in charge or shipped on board.

The date of issuance of the transport document will be deemed to be the date of dispatch, taking in charge or shipped on board, and the date of shipment. However, if the transport document indicates, by stamp or notation, a date of dispatch, taking in charge or shipped on board, this date will be deemed to be the date of shipment.

iii. indicate the place of dispatch, taking in charge or shipment, and the place of final destination stated in the credit, even if:

    a) the transport document states, in addition, a different place of dispatch, taking in charge or shipment or place of final destination, or

    b) the transport document contains the indication 'intended' or similar qualification in relation to the vessel, port of loading or port of discharge.

iv. be the sole original transport document or, if issued in more than one original, be the full set as indicated on the transport document.

v. contain terms and conditions of carriage or make reference to another source containing the terms and conditions of carriage (short form or blank back transport document). Contents of terms and conditions of carriage will not be examined.

vi. contain no indication that it is subject to a charter party.

b. For the purpose of this article, transhipment means unloading from one means of conveyance and reloading to another means of conveyance (whether or not in different modes of transport) during the carriage from the place of dispatch, taking in charge or shipment to the place of final destination stated in the credit.

c. i. A transport document may indicate that the goods will or may be transhipped provided that the entire carriage is covered by one and the same transport document.

   ii. A transport document indicating that transhipment will or may take place is acceptable, even if the credit prohibits transhipment.

Under review:

UCP 600 article 19.a.i

Equivalent article in UCP 500:

UCP 600 article 19.a.i: UCP 500 article 26.i

Analysis:

Article 26 in UCP 500 was reworded as article 19 in UCP 600, but retains the essence of the original. The entire article is thus a revised presentation of article 26 of UCP 500. The word 'multimodal' is no longer the operative term in this revised article. It has been replaced by the description 'covering at least two different modes of transport'. The article carries no major change in implication. Issues worthy of note are as outlined below:

a. This section (article 19.a) deals with two elements, viz., name and signature.

b. The term 'unless otherwise stipulated in the credit' is deleted, since article 1 already contains the provision 'unless expressly modified or excluded.'

c. The expression 'on its face' is deleted (refer to chapter 1, section 1.8.3 for explanation and background to the change).

d. Document requiring name of the carrier ('or multimodal transport operator') is deleted.

e. Name of master not required; text re-worded to read as '...master or a named agent....'.

Further, with regard to the last two sentences beginning with 'Any signature...', the significant issues are as follows:

a. Unlike article 26(a)(i) of UCP 500, there is no reference to a multimodal transport operator; the reference would henceforth only be to the carrier or master

b. Reference to 'authentication' appearing in the beginning ("Any signature or authentication of the carrier or master must be...') as also in the last section ('...an agent signing or authenticating for a carrier...') of article 26(a)(i) of UCP 500 is deleted.

c. In all the articles that refer to transport documents, there is now a consistent approach to the language used in referencing signing and capacity details.

d. No reference to the name of master.

Comments:

All articles on transport document now follow a consistent style of presentation. Of course, the same approach was evident in UCP 500, but it has been further enhanced in UCP 600.

The first sentence of all articles on transport document is modified to read as 'a bill of lading (or, an air transport document, or a non-negotiable bill of lading etc. as applicable), however named, must appear to:....'. In UCP 500 a transport document was described as a 'document, however named...'.

Additionally, the recurrent theme in UCP 500, viz., 'unless otherwise stipulated in the Credit' is completely removed from all sections of the articles on transport documents (as from most parts of the UCP). In view of the stipulation already contained in article 1, there was really no need, even in UCP 500, to include these words. The present deletion takes nothing away from the merit of this version of the UCP.

The Drafting Group was of the view that where the agent signs for the master, the name of the master was not necessary. This position would recur in the other articles related to transport documents.

ISBP 745 articles D1 to D32 present a wide range of issues with regard to multimodal or combined transport documents presented under documentary credits.

ARTICLE 19 (contd. from 19.A.I)

Under review:

Articles 19(a)(ii) to 19(a)(vi)

Equivalent article in UCP 500:

UCP 600 article 19.a.ii: UCP 500 article 26.a.ii

UCP 600 article 19.a.iii: UCP 500 article 26.a.iii (a) and (b)

UCP 600 article 19.a.iv: UCP 500 article 26.a.iv

UCP 600 article 19.a.v: UCP 500 article 26.a.v

UCP 600 article 19.a.vi: UCP 500 article 26.a.vi

Analysis:

UCP 600 article 19.a.ii: '..... at the place stated in the credit...' added. The last section of the article defines how the date of shipment should be interpreted (see comments below).

UCP 600 article 19.a.iii: Text revised, essence retained.

UCP 600 article 19.a.vi: Reference to sail deleted.

Comments:

UCP 600 article 19.a.ii (second section): This section of article 19.ii (beginning with the words 'The date of issuance of the transport...' quoted above) defines what should be taken as the date of shipment. Placing this paragraph as a separate article, or using a sub-heading to indicate the topic would have been justified, given its importance. It would have also helped in easy identification of the subject dealt with here, as also for the ease of cross-reference.

Article numbered 26.a.vii, which is the last article under article 26 in UCP 500 states 'in all other respects meets the stipulation of the credit'. The last article was not carried over to UCP 600 since a presentation must always comply. UCP 600 carries a definition for 'complying presentation'.

ARTICLE 19 (continued from 19.A.VI)

Under review:

Articles 19(b) and 19(c)

Equivalent article in UCP 500:

UCP 600 article 19.b: UCP 500 article 23.b

UCP 600 article 19.c: UCP 500 article 26.b

Analysis: *UCP 600 article 19.b:* article 23(b), UCP 500, has been revised, its scope expanded, and the article redrafted to improve clarity.

UCP 600 article 19.c: article 26(b) in UCP 500 has been broken up into two separate sections or articles. However, the revised article retains the same provisions.

Comments:

UCP 600 article 19.b: In UCP 500, definition of transhipment is available for bill of lading (article 23.b), non-negotiable sea waybill (article 24.b), air transport document (article 27.b) and transportation by road, rail or inland waterway (article 28.b). Although article 26(b) did state that 'even if the Credit prohibits transhipment, banks will accept a multimodal transport document which indicates that transhipment will or may take place', UCP 500 never addressed the issue of 'transhipment' for *multi-modal carriage*. In UCP 600 this has been set right.

+++

ARTICLE 20: BILL OF LADING

a. A bill of lading, however named, must appear to:

   i. indicate the name of the carrier and be signed by:

      - the carrier or a named agent for or on behalf of the carrier, or

      - the master or a named agent for or on behalf of the master.

      Any signature by the carrier, master or agent must be identified as that of the carrier, master or agent.

      Any signature by an agent must indicate whether the agent has signed for or on behalf of the carrier or for or on behalf of the master.

   ii. indicate that the goods have been shipped on board a named vessel at the port of loading stated in the credit by:

      - pre-printed wording, or

      - an on board notation indicating the date on which the goods have been shipped on board.

      The date of issuance of the bill of lading will be deemed to be the date of shipment unless the bill of lading contains an on board notation indicating the date of shipment, in which case the date stated in the on board notation will be deemed to be the date of shipment.

If the bill of lading contains the indication 'intended vessel' or similar qualification in relation to the name of the vessel, an on board notation indicating the date of shipment and the name of the actual vessel is required.

iii. indicate shipment from the port of loading to the port of discharge stated in the credit,

If the bill of lading does not indicate the port of loading stated in the credit as the port of loading, or if it contains the indication 'intended' or similar qualification in relation to the port of loading, an on-board notation indicating the port of loading as stated in the credit, the date of shipment and the name of the vessel is required. This provision also applies even when loading on board or shipment on a named vessel is indicated by pre-printed wording on the bill of lading.

iv. be the sole original bill of lading or, if issued in more than one original, be the full set as indicated on the bill of lading.

v. contain terms and conditions of carriage or make reference to another source containing the terms and conditions of carriage (short form or blank back bill of lading). Contents of terms and conditions of carriage will not be examined.

vi. contain no indication that it is subject to a charter party.

b. For the purpose of this article, transhipment means unloading from one vessel and reloading to another vessel during the carriage from the port of loading to the port of discharge stated in the credit.

c. i. A bill of lading may indicate that the goods will or may be transhipped provided that the entire carriage is covered by one and the same bill of lading.

   ii. A bill of lading indicating that transhipment will or may take place is acceptable, even if the credit prohibits transhipment, if the goods have been shipped in a container, trailer or LASH barge as evidenced by the bill of lading.

d. Clauses in a bill of lading stating that the carrier reserves the right to tranship will be disregarded.

Under review: Article 20

Equivalent article in UCP 500: UCP 600 article 20; UCP 500 article 23

Analysis:

Article 23 in UCP 500 was reworded as article 20, but retains the essence of the original. The entire article is a revised presentation of article 23 of UCP 500. Title of the article modified to 'Bill of Lading'. No major policy changes in this version.

Key points to note are as follows:

- This section of article 20, i.e. article 20(a), deals with two elements, viz., name and signature.
- The term 'unless otherwise stipulated in the credit' (appearing in the first line of article 23(a), UCP 500) has been deleted, since article 1 provides for modifications e.g. 'unless expressly modified or excluded.'
- The expression 'on its face' appearing at the beginning of UCP 500 article 23(a) has been deleted[110].
- Document requiring name of the carrier deleted.

---

[110] Refer to chapter 1, section 1.8.3 for a review of the expression 'on its face'.

- Name of master no longer required; text re-worded to read as '...master or a named agent....'.

Further, with regard to the last two sentences beginning with 'Any signature...', the significant issues are as follows:

- The section 'Any signature or authentication of the carrier or master must be...' has been streamlined, and modified to include 'agent'.
- Reference to 'authentication' appearing in the beginning ("Any signature or authentication of the carrier or master must be...') as also in the last section ('...an agent signing or authenticating for a carrier...') of article 23(a)(i) of UCP 500 has been deleted.
- There is now a consistent approach to the language used in referencing signing and capacity details.

Comments:

Consistency with article 19 in presentation and content should be noted.

The exclusion clause, here as everywhere else, has been dropped in view of the same having been covered under article 1.

At one point early in the rounds of discussions, there was an attempt to define 'bill of lading' (for the purpose of article 2). To the Consulting Group it appeared to be 'an impossible task'. The attempt failed.

ARTICLE 20, BILL OF LADING (analysis contd....)

Under review: UCP 600 article 20.ii to UCP 600 article 20.vi

Equivalent article in UCP 500:

UCP 600 article 20.ii: UCP 500 article 23.ii

UCP 600 article 20.iii: UCP 500 article 23.iii

UCP 600 article 20.iv: UCP 500 article 23.iv

UCP 600 article 20.v: UCP 500 article 23.v

UCP 600 article 20.vi: UCP 500 article 23.vi

Analysis:

UCP 600 article 20.ii: The words: '....at the port of loading stated in the credit...' were added to the earlier article. The remaining section of this article is a continuation of the rest of article 23(ii) in UCP 500, redrafted but only for the sake of clarity.

UCP 600 article 20.iii: The words in article 23(ii), UCP 500, were revised to change the emphasis from negative to positive. '.... The lead sentence in UCP 500 article 23.a.ii, last paragraph viz., 'If the bill of lading indicates a place of receipt or taking in charge different from the port of loading...' now reads as '... If the bill of lading does not indicate the port of loading stated in the credit as the port of loading,…'.

UCP 600 article 20.iv: article 23.a.iv (UCP 500) was reworded; except that, there is no change.

UCP 600 article 20.v: No change.

UCP 600 article 20.a.vi: Earlier reference to 'sailing vessel' in article 23.a.vi (UCP 500) was deleted.

Comments:

UCP 600 article 20.a.ii (last but one section): Placing this subject (about the date of shipment) as a separate article or using a sub-heading to indicate the topic would have helped in easy identification and for purposes of cross-reference.

Article numbered 23.a.vii, which is the last article under article 23 in UCP 500, states 'in all other respects meets the stipulation of the credit'. The last article has not been carried over to UCP 600 since a presentation must be such, anyway. UCP 600 carries a definition for 'complying presentation'.

Article 20.a.iii: An error in grammar in the fourth line of the second paragraph: '…the date of shipment and the name of the vessel *is* required' should be corrected to '*are*' required.

ARTICLE 20, BILL OF LADING (analysis contd....)

Under review: UCP 600 articles 20.b to 20.d

Equivalent article in UCP 500:

UCP 600 article 20.b: UCP 500 article 23.b

UCP 600 article 20.c.i: UCP 500 article 23.c

UCP 600 article 20.c.ii: UCP 500 article 23.d.i

UCP 600 article 20.d: UCP 500 article 23.d.ii

Analysis:

UCP 600 article 20.b: Article 23.b in UCP 500 is reworded, since the sentence in the earlier version ('transhipment means unloading and reloading from one vessel to another vessel') was not grammatically correct.

UCP 600 article 20.c.i: Minor changes in wording.

UCP 600 article 20.c.ii: Minor changes in wording.

Articles 20(c)(i) & 20(c)(ii) provide a window of opportunity for transhipment. In view of this provision in the UCP it is important to note that, *if the issuer wishes to absolutely prohibit or prevent transhipment,* he must specifically prohibit and *exclude article 23(c)(ii)* in a documentary credit. Else, there would always be a possibility that transhipment might take place. (See additional comments below.)

Comments: Article 20(c)(i) above, in its present form serves no purpose that the next article cannot, nor does it appear to make any sense, for it has no relevance as a 'rule'. It does not call for performance or compliance. The sub-section may, therefore, be modified to read as 'A bill of lading indicating that the goods will or may be transhipped is acceptable, provided…' etc.

Further, a careful study will show that articles 20.c.i and 20.c.ii stipulate the same thing, the two convey *exactly the same message*; because 'one and the same bill of lading' in article c(i) and 'a bill of lading' in article (c)(ii) refer to a single (being, just *one*) bill of lading![111]

+++

---

[111] Refer to chapter 3, Note No. 3, section 3.3.9 for more on this subject.

ARTICLE 21: NON-NEGOTIABLE SEA WAYBILL

a. A non-negotiable sea waybill, however named, must appear to:

   i. indicate the name of the carrier and be signed by:

      - the carrier or a named agent for or on behalf of the carrier, or
      - the master or a named agent for or on behalf of the master.

      Any signature by the carrier, master or agent must be identified as that of the carrier, master or agent.

      Any signature by an agent must indicate whether the agent has signed for or on behalf of the carrier or for or on behalf of the master.

   ii. indicate that the goods have been shipped on board a named vessel at the port of loading stated in the credit by:

      - pre-printed wording, or
      - an on board notation indicating the date on which the goods have been shipped on board.

      The date of issuance of the sea waybill will be deemed to be the date of shipment unless the non-negotiable sea waybill contains an on board notation indicating the date of shipment, in which case the date stated in the on board notation will be deemed to be the date of shipment.

If the non-negotiable sea waybill contains the indication 'intended vessel' or similar qualification in relation to the name of the vessel, an on board notation indicating the date of shipment and the name of the actual vessel is required.

iii. indicate shipment from the port of loading to the port of discharge stated in the credit,

If the non-negotiable sea waybill does not indicate the port of loading stated in the credit as the port of loading, or if it contains the indication 'intended' or similar qualification in relation to the port of loading, an on board notation indicating the port of loading as stated in the credit, the date of shipment and the name of the vessel are required. This provision also applies even when loading on board or shipment on a named vessel is indicated by pre-printed wording on the non-negotiable sea waybill.

iv. be the sole original non-negotiable sea waybill or, if issued in more than one original, be the full set as indicated on the non-negotiable sea waybill.

v. contain terms and conditions of carriage or make reference to another source containing the terms and conditions of carriage (short form or blank back non-negotiable sea waybill). Contents of terms and conditions of carriage will not be examined.

vi. contains no indication that it is subject to a charter party.

b. For the purpose of this article, transhipment means unloading from one vessel and reloading to another vessel during the course of carriage from the port of loading to the port of discharge stated in the credit.

c. i. A non-negotiable sea waybill may indicate that the goods will or may be transhipped provided that the entire carriage is covered by one and the same non-negotiable sea waybill.

   ii. A non-negotiable sea waybill indicating that transhipment will or may take place is acceptable, even if the credit prohibits transhipment, if the goods have been shipped in a container, trailer or LASH barge as evidenced by the non-negotiable sea waybill.

d. Clauses in a -negotiable sea waybill stating that the carrier reserves the right to tranship will be disregarded.

Under review: Article 21.a to 21.d

Equivalent article in UCP 500: Article 24

Analysis: The issues are similar to those reviewed under article 20 (Bill of Lading).

Comments: The issues are similar to those reviewed under article 20 (Bill of Lading).

+++

ARTICLE 22: CHARTER PARTY BILL OF LADING:

a. A bill of lading, however named, containing an indication that it is subject to a charter party (charter party bill of lading) must appear to:

   i. be signed by:

      - the master or a named agent for or on behalf of the master, or
      - the owner or a named agent for or on behalf of the owner, or
      - the charterer or a named agent for or on behalf of the charterer.

Any signature by the master, owner, charterer or agent must be identified as that of the master, owner, charterer or agent.

Any signature by an agent must indicate whether the agent has signed for or on behalf of the master, owner or charterer.

An agent signing for or on behalf of the owner or charterer must indicate the name of the owner or charterer.

   ii. indicate that the goods have been shipped on board a named vessel at the port of loading stated in the credit by:

      - pre-printed wording

- an on board notation indicating the date on which the goods have been shipped on board

The date of issuance of the charter party bill of lading will be deemed to be the date of shipment unless the charter party bill of lading contains an on board notation indicating the date of shipment, in which case the date stated in the on board notation will be deemed to be the date of shipment.

iii. indicate shipment from the port of loading to the port of discharge stated in the credit. The port of discharge may also be shown as a range of ports or a geographical area, as stated in the credit.

iv. be the sole original charter party bill of lading or, if issued in more than one original, be the full set as indicated on the charter party bill of lading.

b. A bank will not examine charter party contracts, even if they are required to be presented by the terms of the credit.

Under review: UCP 600 article 22 and UCP 600 article 22.b.

Equivalent article in UCP 500:

UCP 600 article 22: UCP 500 article 25

UCP 600 article 22.a: UCP 500 article 25.a & a.i

UCP 600 article 22.a.i: UCP 500 article 25.a.ii

UCP 600 article 22.a.ii: UCP 500 article 25.a.iv

UCP 600 article 22.a.iii: UCP 500 article 25.a.v

UCP 600 article 22.a.iv: UCP 500 article 25.vi

UCP 600 article 22.b: UCP 500 article 25.b

Analysis:

UCP 600 article 22: The opening section of article 25 in UCP 500 has undergone marginal change in its revised form as article 22(a) in UCP 600. The exclusion clause – here as everywhere else – has been dropped in view of the same having been covered under article 1.

UCP 600 article 22.a.ii: Apart from master, owner and agent (as with other transport documents), 'charterer' was added as the capacity in which a shipper may execute a transport document.

The opening sentence of UCP 500 article 25.a.iv is modified by the addition of the words '... at the port of loading stated in the credit....'. There is no other change in this article.

Observations made earlier under article 20 with regard to 'on its face', authentication, name of master also apply equally well to this section.

UCP 600 article 22.a.iii: The provision contained in article 25(a)(v) of UCP 500 is extended by the addition of the second sentence. Henceforth, a geographical area or region, or a range of ports as ports of discharge would also be acceptable. This provision has been brought in from ISBP, article 106 (refer to article 121 of ISBP 681)[112].

UCP 600 article 22.a. iv: No change from UCP 500 article 25.a.vi.

UCP 600 article 22 (b): Text of article 25.b in UCP 500 modified and refined.

Comments:

Reference to sail in UCP 500 article 25(a)(vii) is deleted. Therefore, there is no reference to 'sail' in UCP 600.

Provision under UCP 500 article 25(a)(viii) was not considered necessary for being carried over owing to the inclusion of the definition of 'complying presentation' in UCP 600.

+++

---

[112] Refer to ISBP 745 article G.9 for the currently operative ICC rule.

ARTICLE 23: AIR TRANSPORT DOCUMENT

a. An air transport document, however named, must appear to:

   i. indicate the name of the carrier and be signed by:

      - the carrier, or
      - a named agent for or on behalf of the carrier.

      Any signature by the carrier or agent must be identified as that of the carrier or agent.

      Any signature by an agent must indicate that the agent has signed for or on behalf of the carrier.

   ii. indicate that the goods have been accepted for carriage.

   iii. indicate the date of issuance. This date will be deemed to be the date of shipment unless the air transport document contains a specific notation of the actual date of shipment, in which case the date stated in the notation will be deemed to be the date of shipment.

      Any other information appearing on the air transport document relative to the flight number and date will not be considered in determining the date of shipment.

   iv. indicate the airport of departure and the airport of destination stated in the credit.

v. be the original for consignor or shipper, even if the credit stipulates a full set of originals.

vi. contain terms and conditions of carriage or make reference to another source containing the terms and conditions of carriage. Contents of terms and conditions of carriage will not be examined.

b. For the purpose of this article, transhipment means unloading from one aircraft and reloading to another aircraft during the carriage from the airport of departure to the airport of destination stated in the credit.

c. i. An air transport document may indicate that the goods will or may be transhipped, provided that the entire carriage is covered by one and the same air transport document.

ii. An air transport document indicating that transhipment will or may take place is acceptable, even if the credit prohibits transhipment.

Under review: Article 23

Equivalent article in UCP 500:

UCP 600 article 23: UCP 500 article 27

UCP 600 article 23.a: UCP 500 article 27.a

UCP 600 article 23.a.i: UCP 500 article 27.a.i

UCP 600 article 23.a.ii: UCP 500 article 27.a.ii

UCP 600 article 23.a.iii: UCP 500 article 27.a.iii

UCP 600 article 23.a.iv: UCP 500 article 27.a.iv

UCP 600 article 23.a.v: UCP 500 article 27.a.v

UCP 600 article 23.a.vi: UCP 500 article 27.a.vi

UCP 600 article 23.b: UCP 500 article 27.b

UCP 600 article 23.c: UCP 500 article 27.c

Analysis:

UCP 600 article 23.a: The exclusion clause appearing in article 27(a) (at the beginning of all transport articles of UCP 500) is dropped, in view of the same having been covered under article 1.

Other observations, in brief are as follows (see comments under articles 19 and 20 for more information):

- Reference to 'on its face' (UCP 500 article 27.a.i) is deleted;

- The reference in article 27(a)(i) to 'authentication' in all its variations is removed;

- Only signing capacities (not authentication) are now included in article 23(a)(i);

UCP 600 article 23.a.iii: Date in a notation will be deemed to be the date of shipment *whether requested by the credit or not* (see additional comments below). Any other information outside the notation, including flight no. and date, will not be considered for determining the date of shipment.

UCP 600 articles 23.a.iv to 23.a.vi: No change.

UCP 600 article 23.b: UCP 500 article 27(b) is reworded. If compared with the version in UCP 600, it will be observed that the structure in the earlier version ('transhipment means unloading and reloading from one vessel to another vessel') was not grammatically correct.

UCP 600 article 23.c: article 27(c) in UCP 500 is reworded.

This sub-article provides a window of opportunity for transhipment. In view of this provision in the UCP, *if the issuer wishes to absolutely prohibit or prevent transhipment,* he must specifically prohibit and *exclude article 23(c)(ii)* in a documentary credit. Else, there would always be a possibility that transhipment may take place. (See additional comments below.)

Comments:

UCP 500 article 27.a.vii is absent in UCP 600 since it is covered by the definition of 'complying presentation'.

Article 23.a.ii (UCP 600) is the same as article no. 149 in ISBP, ICC Publication No. 645 (ISBP 745, article H.7)

There appear to be two changes to policies stated in the ISBP. In the normal course, and as per article 23(a)(iii), UCP 600, the date of issuance of an air transport document would be deemed to be the date of shipment. However, if the air waybill contains a specific notation of the actual date of shipment, the date stated in the notation will be deemed as the date of shipment.

[Article 151 of the ISBP stated that 'If the actual flight date is shown as a separate notation, *but is not required by the credit* (emphasis added), it will be disregarded in determining the date of shipment.] As per the UCP, the exception marked in Italics will no longer be valid. Henceforth, (if not the date of issue) the date in a notation will be the date of shipment, *whether required by the credit or not.* The relevant article, redrafted as article 140 in the revised version of the ISBP (ICC Publication No. 681, which came into effect from 1 July, 2007), has resolved the confusion. (Refer to ISBP 745 article H.18 for the latest interpretation of the rule.)

Article 23.c.i above, in its present form, does not appear to make any sense as it serves no purpose. Suggested modification: 'An air transport document which indicates that the goods will or may be transhipped is acceptable, provided...' etc.

Further, a careful study will show that articles 23.c.i and 23.c.ii carry the same stipulation, the two have exactly the same meaning; because 'one and the same air transport document' in article c.(i) and 'an air transport document' in article c.(ii) refer to a single (being, just one) air transport document![113]

+++

---

[113] Refer to chapter 3, Note No. 3, section 3.3.9 for more on this subject.

ARTICLE 24: ROAD, RAIL OR INLAND WATERWAY TRANSPORT DOCUMENTS

a. A road, rail or inland waterway transport document, however named, must appear to:

   i. indicate the name of the carrier and:

      - be signed by the carrier or a named agent for or on behalf of the carrier, or

      - indicate receipt of the goods by signature, stamp or notation by the carrier or a named agent for or on behalf of the carrier.

   Any signature, stamp or notation of receipt of the goods by the carrier or agent must be identified as that of the carrier or agent.

   Any signature, stamp or notation of receipt of the goods by the agent must indicate that the agent has signed for or on behalf of the carrier.

   If a rail transport document does not identify the carrier, any signature or stamp of the railway company will be accepted as evidence of the document being signed by the carrier.

   ii. indicate the date of shipment or the date the goods have been received for shipment, dispatch or carriage at the place stated in the credit. Unless the transport document contains a dated reception stamp, an indication of the date of receipt or date of shipment, the date of issuance of the transport document will be deemed to be the date of shipment.

iii. indicate the place of shipment and the place of destination stated in the credit.

b. i. A road transport document must appear to be the original for consignor or shipper or bear no marking indicating for whom the document has been prepared.

ii. A rail transport document marked 'duplicate' will be accepted as an original.

iii. The rail or inland waterway transport document will be accepted as an original whether marked as an original or not.

c. In the absence of an indication on the transport document as to the number of originals issued, the number presented will be deemed to constitute a full set.

d. For the purpose of this article, transhipment means unloading and reloading from one means of conveyance to another means of conveyance, within the same mode of transport, during the course of carriage from the place of shipment to the place of destination stated in the credit.

e. i. A road, rail or inland waterway transport document may indicate that the goods will or may be transhipped provided that the entire carriage is covered by one and the same air transport document.

ii. A road, rail or inland waterway transport document indicating that transhipment will or may take place is acceptable, even if the credit prohibits transhipment.

Under review: UCP 600 articles 24.a to 24.e

Equivalent article in UCP 500:

UCP 600 article 24: UCP 500 article 28

UCP 600 article 24.a.i: UCP 500 article 28.a.i

UCP 600 article 24.a.ii: UCP 500 article 28.a.ii

UCP 600 article 24.a.iii: UCP 500 article 28.a.iii

UCP 600 article 24.b: UCP 500 article 28.b (part)

UCP 600 article 24.c: UCP 500 article 28.b

UCP 600 article 24.d: UCP 500 article 28.c

UCP 600 article 24.e: UCP 500 article 28.d

Analysis:

UCP 600 article 24.a & a.i: The exclusion clause appearing in article 28.a is dropped since it is already covered under article 1. Reference to 'on its face' (UCP 500 article 28.a.i, first line) is deleted. The reference to 'authentication' in article 28.a.i. is deleted at all places.

UCP 600 article 24.a.i: Only signing capacities (not authentication) are now included in this section. Article 24.a.i outlines the signing requirements and capacity identification.

UCP 600 article 24.ii: The words were revised to capture reception stamp, date of receipt or date of shipment.

UCP 600 article 24.iii: No change from UCP 500.

UCP 600 article 24.b.i, ii & iii: The second sentence of UCP 500 article 28.b pertaining to original document(s) has been broken up in to three distinct sub-paragraphs for the separate purposes of (a) road transport (24.b.i), (b) carriage by rail (24.b.ii), and (c) rail or inland waterway transport (24.b.iii).

UCP 600 articles 24.c, 24.d and 24.e: The articles are reworded, but there is no change worthy of note.

Comments:

UCP 500 article 28.iv not retained since the term 'complying presentation' covers the issue.

The comments against the analysis of UCP 600 article 23.c.ii may be referred to.

+++

ARTICLE 25: COURIER, POST RECEIPTS OR CERTIFICATE OF POSTING

a. A courier receipt, however named, evidencing receipt of goods for transport, must appear to:

   i. indicate the name of the courier service and be stamped or signed by the named courier service at the place from which the credit states the goods are to be shipped; and

   ii. indicate a date of pickup or of receipt or wording to this effect. This date will be deemed to be the date of shipment.

b. A requirement that courier charges are to be paid or prepaid may be satisfied by a transport document issued by a courier service evidencing that courier charges are for the account of a party other than the consignee.

c. A post receipt or certificate of posting, however named, evidencing receipt of goods for transport, must appear to be stamped or signed and dated at the place from which the credit states the goods are to be shipped. This date will be deemed to be the date of shipment.

Under review: Article 25

Equivalent article in UCP 500:

UCP 600 article 25: UCP 500 article 29

UCP 600 article 25.a.i: UCP 500 article 29.b.i

UCP 600 article 25.a.ii: UCP 500 article 29.b.ii

UCP 600 article 25.b: New

UCP 600 article 25.c: UCP 500 article 29.a.i and ii

Analysis: 'Certificate of Posting' added to the title and to the existing provisions.

UCP 600 article 25.a.i and ii: UCP 500 article 29.b.I & ii is reworded and modified. It now covers receipt of goods for transport. 'Expedited delivery service' is removed. The term 'on its face' and reference to authentication were deleted.

UCP 500 article 29.a.ii is already covered in article 1; therefore, not repeated in this section under UCP 600.

UCP 600 article 25.b: New provision.

UCP 600 article 25.c: Covers despatch by post.

Comments: UCP 500 article 29.b.iii deleted due to the inclusion of the expression 'complying presentation' in UCP 600. Exclusion clause covered in article 1; deleted from the revised version.

+++

ARTICLE 26: 'ON DECK', 'SHIPPER'S LOAD AND COUNT', 'SAID BY SHIPPER TO CONTAIN' AND CHARGES ADDITIONAL TO FREIGHT

a. A transport document must not indicate that the goods are or will be loaded on deck. A clause on a transport document stating that the goods may be loaded on deck is acceptable.

b. A transport document bearing such clauses as 'shipper's load and count' and 'said by shipper to contain' is acceptable.

c. A transport document may bear a reference, by stamp or otherwise, to charges additional to freight.

Under review: Article 26

Equivalent article in UCP 500:

UCP 600 article 26.a: UCP 500 article 31.i.

UCP 600 article 26.b: UCP 500 article 31.ii.

UCP 600 article 26.c: UCP 500 article 33.d

Analysis: Exclusion clause ('unless otherwise stipulated in the credit') deleted.

The term 'on the face' in article 31.ii of UCP 500 is deleted. The three issues covered in this article are as follows:

1. On Deck

In many ways article UCP 600 article 26(a) is an odd article, because the first part of the article requires that a “transport document must not indicate that the goods are or will be loaded on deck”. The reality is that a majority of goods are shipped above deck (especially today’s container vessels). Having stipulated thus, it immediately reverses its stand and states that, “A clause on a transport document stating that the goods may be loaded on deck is acceptable.” The difference? It’s between ‘will’ and ‘may’.

2. 'Shipper’s Load and Count'/Said by Shipper to Contain'

These are important provisions – especially in container transportation of cargo, where the containers are locked and sealed much before being loaded on board. These are general statements, but absolve the carrier of certain responsibilities with regard to the cargo.

3. 'Charges Additional to Freight'

The provision is a simplified version of UCP 500, article 33(d), which indicates that a transport document may bear a reference to charges additional to the freight. This issue, tiled “Freight and additional costs” is also covered in ISBP 745 under articles E26, E27, F24, F25, G24, G25, H25, H26 and J20.

Comments:

A small segment of article 33, viz., article 33.d, was carried over from UCP 500 and retained in the form of UCP 600 article 26.c. The rest of UCP 500 article 33 was dropped.

+++

ARTICLE 27: CLEAN TRANSPORT DOCUMENT

A bank will only accept a clean transport document. A clean transport document is one bearing no clause or notation expressly declaring a defective condition of the goods or their packaging. The word 'clean' need not appear on a transport document, even if a credit has a requirement for that transport document to be 'clean on board'.

Under review: Article 27

Equivalent article in UCP 500: Article 32

Analysis: Three separate articles in UCP 500 viz., articles 32.a, 32.b & 32.c have now been collated and compressed into this single article.

UCP 500 article 32.b had provided for acceptance by banks of 'claused' transport documents through a provision in this article by saying, 'Banks will not accept... unless the Credit expressly stipulates the clauses or notations which may be accepted.' Here, in article 27 of UCP 600, that window stands firmly and decisively closed. The carrier would have to state clearly and with finality if, for example, the packaging is sea-worthy or not. A bank will only accept a *clean* transport document.

The word 'clean' need not appear on a transport document.

Comments: UCP 500 article 32.c: Not necessary due to definition of 'complying presentation'.

ARTICLE 28, INSURANCE DOCUMENT AND COVERAGE:

a. An insurance document, such as an insurance policy, an insurance certificate or a declaration under an open cover, must appear to be issued and signed by an insurance company, an underwriter or their agents or their proxies.

   Any signature by an agent or proxy must indicate whether the agent or proxy has signed for or on behalf of the insurance company or underwriter.

b. When the insurance document indicates that it has been issued in more than one original, all originals must be presented.

c. Cover notes will not be accepted.

d. An insurance policy is acceptable in lieu of an insurance certificate or a declaration under an open cover.

e. The date of the insurance document must be no later than the date of shipment, unless it appears from the insurance document that the cover is effective from a date no later than the date of shipment.

f. i. The insurance document must indicate the amount of insurance coverage and be in the same currency as the credit.

   ii. A requirement in the credit for insurance coverage to be for a percentage of the value of the goods, of the invoice value or similar is deemed to be the minimum amount of coverage required.

If there is no indication in the credit of the insurance coverage required, the amount of insurance coverage must be at least 110% of the CIF or CIP value of the goods.

When the CIF or CIP value cannot be determined from the documents, the minimum insurance coverage must be calculated on the basis of the amount for which honour or negotiation is requested or the gross value of the goods as shown in the invoice, whichever is greater.

iii. The insurance document must indicate that the risks are covered at least between the place of taking in charge or shipment and the place of discharge or final destination as stated in the credit.

g. A credit should state the type of insurance required and, if any, the additional risks to be covered. Imprecise terms such as ‘usual risks’ or ‘customary risks’ shall be disregarded, and an insurance document will be accepted without regard to any risks that are not covered.

h. When a credit requires insurance against ‘all risks’ and an insurance document is presented containing any 'all risks' notation or clause, whether or not bearing the heading 'all risks', the insurance document will be accepted without regard to any risks stated to be excluded.

i. An insurance document may contain reference to any exclusion clause.

j. An insurance document may indicate that the cover is subject to a franchise or excess (deductible).

Under review: Article 28.a to 28.e.

Equivalent article in UCP 500: UCP 600 article 28: UCP 500 articles 34, 35 & 36

UCP 600 article 28.a: UCP 500 article 34.a

UCP 600 article 28.b: UCP 500 article 34.b

UCP 600 article 28.c: UCP 500 article 34.c

UCP 600 article 28.d: UCP 500 article 34.d

UCP 600 article 28.e: UCP 500 article 34.e

Analysis:

General observations: articles 34, 35 and 36 of UCP 500 have been brought together in this single article of UCP 600.

Almost every article in article 34, UCP 500 relating to insurance contained the term '....unless authorised in the credit'. This expression was removed from these articles while revising and carrying them over to UCP 600. This step is in line with similar revisions at other places in UCP 600.

UCP 600 article 28.a: The term 'proxy' has been introduced to reflect another signing authority. Hence, the reference to agents in UCP 500 article 34(a) and 34(d) was expanded to include agents or proxies.

The term 'on its face' (UCP 500 article 34.a) deleted in accordance with general consensus of Drafting Group.

Insurance documents have been described including declaration under open cover.

Signing conditions have been modified to bring them in line with, and to have a structure, that are similar to those applicable to transport documents.

UCP 600 article 28.b: From UCP 500 article 34(b), the term '....unless authorised in the credit' has been removed. Therefore, all originals *must* be presented, without exception (unless article 1 is activated).

UCP 600 article 28.c: The clause in UCP 500 article 34(c) had read 'cover notes issued by brokers will not be accepted, unless specifically authorised in the credit'. The provision 'issued by broker' has now been deleted. Therefore, this provision in UCP 600 will be final and binding, irrespective of whether the issuer is a broker or otherwise (say, by the insurance company itself). No cover notes will be accepted, period.

From article 34.c of UCP 500 on cover note, the exception clause, viz., 'unless specifically authorised in the credit' is removed.

UCP 600 article 28.d: This is a simplified version of UCP 500 article 34.d. The subject of pre-signed certificate or declaration finds no mention in the UCP 600.

UCP 600 article 28.e: Introduction of the word 'shipment' simplifies this article.

Comments:

A requirement in the LC for certain insurance coverage is understood as the 'minimum' insurance coverage. If the LC is silent on this matter then a minimum of CIP/CIF value plus 10 per cent is required.

ISBP 745 articles K1 to K21 supplements UCP 600 and provides additional guidance with regard to insurance document and coverage.

ARTICLE 28 (analysis contd....)

Article 28.f.i to 28.j

Equivalent article in UCP 500:

- UCP 600 article 28.f.i & ii : UCP 500 article 34.f.i & ii
- UCP 600 article 28.f.iii : New
- UCP 600 article 28.g : UCP 500 article 35.a & b

- UCP 600 article 28.h : UCP 500 article 36
- UCP 600 article 28.i : UCP 500 article 35.a
- UCP 600 article 28.j : UCP 500 article 34.a

Analysis:

UCP 600 article 28.f: articles 34.f.i and 34.f.ii in UCP 500 are restructured for clarity in meaning and expression.

As stated earlier, the clause '...unless otherwise stipulated in the credit...' is deleted from UCP 600. The requirement of 'same currency as the credit' would be applicable unless specifically waived by the issuer.

UCP 600 article 28.f.iii: New provision; the stipulation that 'insurance must be covered at least between the two places/ports/airports stated in the credit' was not mentioned in UCP 500.

UCP 600 article 28.g: No change.

UCP 600 article 28.h: No change from article 36 (UCP 500); banks will accept insurance documents with any exclusion clause.

UCP 600 article 28.j: 'Unless otherwise stipulated in the Credit...' deleted.

Comments:

None.

+++

ARTICLE 29: EXTENSION OF EXPIRY DATE OR LAST DAY FOR PRESENTATION

a. If the expiry date of a credit or the last day for presentation falls on a day when the bank to which presentation is to be made is closed for reasons other than those referred to in article 36, the expiry date or the last day for presentation, as the case may be, will be extended to the first following banking day.

b. If presentation is made on the first following banking day, a nominated bank must provide the issuing bank or confirming bank with a statement on its covering schedule that the presentation was made within the time limits extended in accordance with article 29(a).

c. The latest date for shipment shall not be extended as a result of article 29 (a).

Under review:

Article 29

Equivalent article in UCP 500:

UCP 600 article 29: UCP 500 article 44

UCP 600 article 29.a: UCP 500 article 44.a

UCP 600 article 29.b: UCP 500 article 44.c

UCP 600 article 29.c: UCP 500 article 44.b

Analysis:

UCP 600 article 29.a: No change.

UCP 600 article 29.b: The mode or *place* (how or where) for providing the required 'statement that the documents were presented within the time limit extended... ' had not been stipulated in UCP 500 article 44.c. UCP 600 now stipulates that the information required to comply with the provisions of this article should appear *on the covering schedule* of the nominated bank.

UCP 600 article 29.c: UCP 500 article 44.b reduced and simplified. The second part of article 44.b has been deleted from this section, since it is covered by article 6 in UCP 600.

Comments:

None.

+++

ARTICLE 30: TOLERANCE IN CREDIT AMOUNT, QUANTITY AND UNIT PRICES

a. The words 'about' or 'approximately' used in connection with the amount of the credit or the quantity or the unit price stated in the credit are to be construed as allowing a tolerance not to exceed 10% more or 10% less than the amount, the quantity or the unit price to which they refer.

b. A tolerance not to exceed 5% more or 5% less than the quantity of the goods is allowed, provided that the credit does not state the quantity in terms of a stipulated number of packing units or individual items and the total amount of the drawings does not exceed the amount of the credit.

c. Even when partial shipments are not allowed, a tolerance not to exceed 5% less than the amount of the credit is allowed, provided that the quantity of the goods, if stated in the credit, is shipped in full and a unit price, if stated in the credit, is not reduced or that article 30 (b) is not applicable. This tolerance does not apply when the credit stipulates a specific tolerance or uses the expressions referred to in article 30 (a).

Under review:

Article 30

Equivalent article in UCP 500:

UCP 600 article 30: UCP 500 article 39

UCP 600 article 30.a: UCP 500 article 39.a

UCP 600 article 30.b: UCP 500 article 39.b

UCP 600 article 30.c: UCP 500 article 39.c

Analysis:

UCP 600 article 30.a: No significant change. The terms 'circa' and 'or similar expressions' have been deleted. The word 'circa' is not seen nowadays; the term 'or similar expressions' is irrelevant and vague. The two options that are commonly used and are quoted more often are 'about' and 'approximately'. These two have been retained.

UCP 600 article 30.b: Language simplified; no significant change. A variation of 5 per cent in quantity is allowed. This is usually used for bulk situations, where the quantity may vary for good reasons.

UCP 600 article 30.c: Simplified, no change in meaning; principle applies whether partial shipment allowed or not. The variation refers to the amount and is usually used in a CIP/CIF situation where the amount includes an estimated freight amount/insurance premium that turns out to be lower than expected.

Comments: This article is still one of the most intriguing. Some are still unable to wrap their heads around it.

ARTICLE 31, PARTIAL DRAWINGS OR SHIPMENTS

a. Partial drawings or shipments are allowed.

b. A presentation consisting of more than one set of transport documents evidencing shipment commencing on the same means of conveyance and for the same journey, provided they indicate the same destination, will not be regarded as covering a partial shipment, even if they indicate different dates of shipment or different ports of loading, places of taking in charge or dispatch. If the presentation consists of more than one set of transport documents, the latest date of shipment as evidenced on any of the sets of transport documents will be regarded as the date of shipment.

   A presentation consisting of more than one set of transport documents evidencing shipment on more than one means of conveyance within the same mode of transport will be regarded as covering a partial shipment, even if the means of conveyance leave on the same day for the same destination.

c. A presentation consisting of more than one courier receipt, post receipt or certificate of posting will not be regarded as a partial shipment if the courier receipts, post receipts or certificates of posting appear to have been stamped or signed by the same courier or postal service at the same place and date and for the same destination.

Under review: Article 31

Equivalent article in UCP 500:

UCP 600 article 31: UCP 500 article 40

UCP 600 article 31.a: UCP 500 article 40.a

UCP 600 article 31.b: UCP 500 article 40.b

UCP 600 article 31.c: UCP 500 article 40.c

Analysis:

UCP 600 article 31.a: The expression 'unless the Credit stipulates otherwise' which comprises the rest of this article (article 40.a. UCP 500) is deleted. Obviously, if the credit did not permit partial shipment, this provision would not be valid.

UCP 600 article 31.b: No change in meaning. The article provides an addition by way of clarification that, in the case of multiple presentations on same mode, the latest date on any of the sets of transport document would be construed as the 'date of shipment'. (This is in line with equivalent provisions in the ISBP)[114].

The term 'partial shipment' has been clearly defined (article 31.b, second paragraph). The same paragraph also defines partial shipment where more than one mode

---

[114] ISBP 745 article C15.

is used. This is a new provision, and a useful clarification, that has been added to UCP 600.

UCP 600 article 31.c: No change. 'Dispatch notes' have been deleted (as they have in the article for 'Post and Courier receipts') on account of limited or no usage in practice.

Comments:

'Partial drawings' in the UCP also accommodates the situations where the UCP 600 is being applied to a standby LC.

+++

ARTICLE 32: INSTALMENT DRAWINGS OR SHIPMENTS

If a drawing or shipment by instalments within given periods is stipulated in the credit and any instalment is not drawn or shipped within the period allowed for that instalment, the credit ceases to be available for that and any subsequent instalment.

Under review:

Article 32

Equivalent article in UCP 500:

Article 41.

Analysis:

No change.

Comments:

The difference between partial shipment and instalment shipment should be very carefully noted. Additional information is available at ISBP 745 article C15.

+++

ARTICLE 33: HOURS OF PRESENTATION:

A bank has no obligation to accept a presentation outside of its banking hours.

Under review: Article 33

Equivalent article in UCP 500: Article 45.

Analysis:

No change, except that the word 'Banks' has been changed to 'A bank'.

Comments:

ICC Opinion TA635Rev states the following:

> *"... whether or not a presentation is allowed to be made outside the banking hours of the trade department of a bank is for that bank to decide. Article 33 allows a nominated bank or issuing bank to decide whether or not it will accept a presentation made by a presenter outside of its banking hours. .....*
>
> *.....A bank that receives documents on a day when the mail receiving unit is working, but the trade department is not, may decide to acknowledge receipt of the documents but on the basis that they are considered as having been received for the next working day of the trade department...."*

It may be too much to expect the 'inward mail department' or the security staff on duty to, "acknowledge receipt of the documents on the basis that they are considered as having been received for the next working day of the trade department." A seal with an appropriate narration could possibly address the issue.

+++

ARTICLE 34, DISCLAIMER ON EFFECTIVENESS OF DOCUMENTS

A bank assumes no liability or responsibility for the form, sufficiency, accuracy, genuineness, falsification or legal effect of any document, or for the general or particular conditions stipulated in a document or superimposed thereon; nor does it assume any liability or responsibility for the description, quantity, weight, quality, condition, packing, delivery, value or existence of the goods, services or other performances represented by any document, or for the good faith or acts or omissions, solvency, performance or standing of the consignor, the carrier, the forwarder, the consignee or the insurer of the goods or any other person.

Under review: Article 34

Equivalent article in UCP 500: Article 15.

Analysis: No change, except minor modification to reflect 'singular' usage of the word 'Bank'. The term '.... services or other performances...' added to bring the article in line with article 5.

Comments:

None.

+++

ARTICLE 35, DISCLAIMER ON TRANSMISSION AND TRANSLATION

A bank assumes no liability or responsibility for the consequences arising out of delay, loss in transit, mutilation or other errors arising in the transmission of any messages or delivery of letters or documents, when such messages, letters or documents are transmitted or sent according to the requirements stated in the credit, or when the bank may have taken the initiative in the choice of the delivery service in the absence of such instructions in the credit.

If a nominated bank determines that a presentation is complying and forwards the documents to the issuing bank or confirming bank, whether or not the nominated bank has honoured or negotiated, an issuing bank or confirming bank must honour or negotiate, or reimburse that nominated bank, even when the documents have been lost in transit between the nominated bank and the issuing bank or confirming bank, or between the confirming bank and the issuing bank.

A bank assumes no liability or responsibility for errors in translation or interpretation of technical terms and may transmit credit terms without translating them.

Under review: Article 35

Equivalent article in UCP 500: Article 16.

Analysis:

Article 35 is a central disclaimer article in UCP 600. It declines to accept responsibility of the involved banks in certain situations.

The two sentences that made up UCP 500 article 16 are now split. Transmission and translation are two separate topics that now appear in two completely separate sentences (refer to the first and last paragraphs respectively).

The second paragraph of this article, beginning with 'If a nominated bank....', is a new provision, placing responsibility on a bank for the first time ever for documents lost in transit. The article provides that reimbursement may be effected based on copies or *replaced* original documents.

The last sentence in article 16 (UCP 500) was rephrased and separately stated as the last paragraph in this revised article.

The article consists of three parts[115]:

The first part deals with a situation where a bank has followed the instructions received or, in the absence of any instruction, when the bank itself has taken the

---

[115] This section sourced from TSU.

initiative to forward the documents. Where the bank deviates from the instruction received, it is liable and responsible for the consequences arising out of the same. For example, if the L/C calls for a specific courier service to forward the documents, and the nominated bank chooses a different courier service then the nominated faces the risk if the documents are lost in transit. (However, the fact that a different courier service was chosen is no reason for the issuing bank to refuse the documents. If a complying presentation is made to the issuing bank, then it is obligated to honour.)

The second part deals with documents lost in transit between (a) a nominated bank and an issuing bank or a confirming bank, or (b) a confirming bank and an issuing bank. It covers the following situations:

1. Where the nominated bank determines that the presentation is complying, and forwards the documents to the issuing or confirming bank, the risk of documents lost in transit lies with the issuing/confirming bank.
2. Where the nominated bank determines that the presentation is NOT complying, and forwards the documents to the issuing or confirming bank, the risk of documents lost in transit does not lie with the issuing/confirming bank.
3. Where the nominated bank has not examined the presentation but forwards the documents to the issuing or confirming bank, the risk of documents

> lost in transit does not lie with the issuing/confirming bank.

In respect of the situation where the documents are lost in transit ICC Opinion TA.639rev should be noted. It includes the following statement:

> "Where only one mailing is made, and this was requested in the credit or no indication of the number of mailings was given and documents are lost in transit, the issuing or confirming bank may determine that they require a presentation to be re-created consisting of copies of the documents that were originally presented."

In other words, a nominated bank may have to prove that the documents did comply by providing copies of documents to the issuing or the confirming bank.

The third and last part states that a bank assumes no liability or responsibility for errors in translation or interpretation of technical terms and may transmit credit terms without translating them. This also means that the bank has no obligation to translate the L/C terms. So for example if a nominated bank received an L/C in a language it does not understand, it may translate it (subject to the provisions in this article) or it may choose to forward it 'as received'.

Comments: The title of this article has been modified; 'and Translation' has been added to the title to reflect the inclusion of 'translation' in the content of this article.

In the light of the many 'disclaimers' in the UCP, this is the first instance where a bank is being made responsible for an event. This article now offers to the beneficiary protection against documents lost in transit after the documents have been presented to a nominated bank.

+++

ARTICLE 36: FORCE MAJEURE

A bank assumes no liability or responsibility for the consequences arising out of the interruption of its business by Acts of God, riots, civil commotions, insurrections, wars, acts of terrorism, or by any strikes or lockouts or any other causes beyond its control.

A bank will not, upon resumption of its business, honour or negotiate under a credit that expired during such interruption of its business.

Under review: Article 36

Equivalent article in UCP 500: Article 17.

Analysis:

Only minor changes have been effected. 'Acts of terrorism' has been added as a 'force majeure' event.

The provision 'unless specifically authorised…' appearing at the beginning of the second paragraph in UCP 500 article 17 has been deleted in UCP 600. No exceptions would, therefore, be permitted.

Comments:

ICC National Committees were offered two options. One was this version, plus another one allowing 5 days' margin after bank re-opened. The version that now exists in this article was finally chosen.

Long after this article found a place in the UCP, the covid-19 pandemic that struck the world in late 2019 brought the issue of force majeure to the fore. The problem issues included the inability to present to a nominated bank, presentation in digitised format, change of a nominated bank, the lack of postal or courier service for the despatch of the documents, complete closure of air transport between countries, closure of banks and businesses by government order and so on. The ICC came out with a series of circulars on Force Majeure, which included the following:

a. ICC Force Majeure Clause 2003; ICC Publication No. 650

b. ICC Force Majeure and Hardship Clauses March 2020

c. ICC Guidance paper on the impact of COVID-19 on trade finance transactions issued subject to ICC rules (no date of issue, no reference number)

d. ICC Force majeure clauses in commercial contracts - General considerations (no date of issue, no reference number)

e. Digital rapid response measures taken by banks under covid-19; Author: ICC Digitalisation Working Group1

+++

ARTICLE 37: DISCLAIMER FOR ACTS OF AN INSTRUCTED PARTY

a. A bank utilizing the services of another bank for the purpose of giving effect to the instructions of the applicant does so for the account and at the risk of the applicant.

b. An issuing bank or advising bank assumes no liability or responsibility should the instructions it transmits to another bank not be carried out, even if it has taken the initiative in the choice of that other bank.

c. A bank instructing another bank to perform services is liable for any commissions, fees, costs or expenses ('charges') incurred by that bank in connection with its instructions.

   If a credit states that charges are for the account of the beneficiary and charges cannot be collected or deducted from proceeds, the issuing bank remains liable for payment of charges.

   A credit or amendment should not stipulate that the advising to a beneficiary is conditional upon the receipt by the advising bank or second advising bank of its charges.

d. The applicant shall be bound by and liable to indemnify a bank against all obligations and responsibilities imposed by foreign laws and usages.

Under review: Article 37

Equivalent article in UCP 500:

UCP 600 article 37: UCP 500 article 18

UCP 600 article 37.a: UCP 500 article 18.a

UCP 600 article 37.b: UCP 500 article 18.b

UCP 600 article 37.c: UCP 500 article 18.c

UCP 600 article 37.d: UCP 500 article 18.d

Analysis:

UCP 600 article 37.a: No change.

UCP 600 article 37.b: The word 'banks' at the beginning of article 18(b) in UCP 500 was replaced with 'an issuing bank or advising bank...'. 'Banks' (in UCP 500) is now defined as the issuing bank or advising bank since, in credit operations, not all banks are required to transmit instructions at the instance of another bank.

UCP 600 article 37.c: The word 'party' in UCP 500 article 18(c) is replaced with 'bank' or 'beneficiary', as applicable[116].

The last segment of article 37.c beginning with the words 'A credit or amendment should not stipulate that the advising to a beneficiary...' etc. enumerates a new rule covering issuance of LCs with request for charges to be collected in advance. What has been emphasised is that

---

[116]Refer to note on this subject in chapter 1, section 1.8.4.

payment (or recovery) of charges should not be linked to the act of advising a credit or an amendment.

UCP 600 article 37.d: No change.

Comments: *Sub-section 37.c, first and second paragraphs:* The contents of the first and the second paragraphs should have been placed under a separate article titled 'Charges'. The contents of these paragraphs have nothing in common with the title of this article or with the thrust of sub-sections 37.a and 37.b.

Sub-section 37.c, third paragraph: The third paragraph, beginning with the words 'A credit or amendment should not...etc.' should be removed from this position in the UCP and placed under article 9. The contents and the purpose of this portion of sub-section 37.c is not in any way related to the preceding sections of this article, and appears irrelevant at this place. On the contrary, it is directly connected with advising of credits and amendments.

Background to third paragraph, sub-section 37.c: Though no commentary or explanation is available till date, it is not very difficult to surmise the compulsions behind the framing of this rule. Another unhealthy practice, a new way to 'improve' on the rules of the UCP would, in all probability, have been devised by certain enterprising banks. There was the need for a specific rule to put a stop to these 'innovations'.

+++

ARTICLE 38: TRANSFERABLE CREDITS

a. A bank is under no obligation to transfer a credit except to the extent and in the manner expressly consented to by that bank.

b. For the purpose of this article:

   Transferable credit means a credit that specifically states it is 'transferable'. A transferable credit may be made available in whole or in part to another beneficiary ('second beneficiary') at the request of the beneficiary ('first beneficiary').

   Transferring bank means a nominated bank that transfers the credit or, in a credit available with any bank, a bank that is specifically authorized by the issuing bank to transfer and that transfers the credit. An issuing bank may be a transferring bank.

   Transferred credit means a credit that has been made available by the transferring bank to a second beneficiary.

c. Unless otherwise agreed at the time of transfer, all charges (such as commissions, fees, costs or expenses) incurred in respect of a transfer must be paid by the first beneficiary.

d. A credit may be transferred in part to more than one second beneficiary provided partial drawings or shipments are allowed.

A transferred credit cannot be transferred at the request of a second beneficiary to any subsequent beneficiary. The first beneficiary is not considered to be a subsequent beneficiary.

e. Any request for transfer must indicate if and under what conditions amendments may be advised to the second beneficiary. The transferred credit must clearly indicate those conditions.

f. If a credit is transferred to more than one second beneficiary, rejection of an amendment by one or more second beneficiary does not invalidate the acceptance by any other second beneficiary, with respect to which the transferred credit will be amended accordingly. For any second beneficiary that rejected the amendment, the transferred credit will remain unamended.

g. The transferred credit must accurately reflect the terms and conditions of the credit, including confirmation, if any, with the exception of:

- the amount of the credit,
- any unit price stated therein,
- the expiry date,
- the period for presentation,
- the latest shipment date or given period for shipment,

any or all of which may be reduced or curtailed.

The percentage for which insurance cover must be effected may be increased to provide the amount of cover stipulated in the credit or in these articles.

The name of the first beneficiary may be substituted for that of the applicant in the credit.

If the name of the applicant is specifically required by the credit to appear in any document other than the invoice, such requirement must be reflected in the transferred credit.

h. The first beneficiary has the right to substitute its own invoice and draft, if any, for those of a second beneficiary for an amount not in excess of that stipulated in the credit, and upon such substitution the first beneficiary can draw under the credit for the difference, if any, between its invoice and the invoice of a second beneficiary.

i. If the first beneficiary is to present its own invoice and draft, if any, but fails to do so on first demand, or if the invoices presented by the first beneficiary creates discrepancies that did not exist in the presentation made by the second beneficiary and the first beneficiary fails to correct them on first demand, the transferring bank has the right to present the documents as received from the second beneficiary to the issuing bank, without further responsibility to the first beneficiary.

j. The first beneficiary may, in its request for transfer, indicate that honour or negotiation is to be effected to a second beneficiary at the place to which the credit has been transferred, up to and including the expiry date of the credit. This is without prejudice to the right of the first beneficiary in accordance with article 38(h).

k. Presentation of documents by or on behalf of a second beneficiary must be made to the transferring bank.

Under review: Article 38.a to 38.d

Equivalent article in UCP 500:

UCP 600 article 38: UCP 500 article 48

UCP 600 article 38.a: UCP 500 article 48.c

UCP 600 article 38.b: UCP 500 article 48.a & b

UCP 600 article 38.c: UCP 500 article 48.f

UCP 600 article 38.d: UCP 500 article 48.g

Analysis:

UCP 600 article 38.a: article 48.c of UCP 500 was rescued from the middle in UCP 500 where it was submerged and lost, and moved to its primary position at the top of this article. Article 48.c (UCP 500) now forms the basis for article 38(a) (UCP 600) being the pivotal stipulation and accordingly deserves proper emphasis.

UCP 600 article 38.b: Articles 48(a) & 48(b) in UCP 500 were reworded and restructured. Definitions form the crux of this sub-section. The definition of a 'transferring bank' was shifted from article 48.a (UCP 500) to the next article (article 38.b in UCP 600) and separately stated. New definition added - 'Transferred Credit' is clearly defined.

Through suitable modification and re-drafting, an issuing bank's capacity to transfer is clarified in this section.

This sub-section contains mostly clarifications and rearrangements, but there is no significant change in meaning or interpretation from that in the original clauses in UCP 500.

(a) *UCP 600 article 38.c:* No change.

(b) *UCP 600 article 38.d:* article 48(g) of UCP 500 was redrafted for clarity. The words 'unless otherwise stated in the Credit...' at the beginning of this article were deleted.

Transferable LCs should not provide for more than one transfer, that being the rule earlier anyway, has now been stated in clear terms that are easily understandable. The modification removes the inherent contradiction caused by the phrase 'unless otherwise...' of the article in UCP 500, and also helps to project a clear meaning of the words 'can be transferred once only'.

Comments: Formal definitions have now been provided for the terms transferable credit, transferred credit and transferring bank (as mentioned under comments for article 2 - Definitions).

These definitions are placed under article 38 ('Transferable Credit') and not under article 2 as was done for all other terms that were similarly defined. The Drafting Group felt that the transferable credit was not a standard offering, but was an instrument in its own right. Therefore, the view was that an article on transferable credits should be self-containing and be presented separately, on a stand-alone basis.

ARTICLE 38: TRANSFERABLE CREDITS (analysis contd....)

Under review: Articles 38.e to 38.k

Equivalent article in UCP 500:

UCP 600 article 38.e: UCP 500 article 48.d

UCP 600 article 38.f: UCP 500 article 48.e

UCP 600 article 38.g: UCP 500 article 48.h

UCP 600 article 38.h: UCP 500 article 48.g

UCP 600 article 38.i: UCP 500 article 48.f

UCP 600 article 38.j: UCP 500 article 48.j

UCP 600 article 38.k: UCP 500 article 48.j

Analysis: *UCP 600 article 38.e:* The requirement for 'irrevocable' instructions (mentioned in article 48.d of UCP 500) regarding amendments is deleted.

UCP 600 article 38.f: No change.

UCP 600 article 38.g: No major change, except the addition of the words 'including confirmation' in the operative part of the article. This addition was necessary to ensure that the *transferred credit* truly reflected *all* the terms of the original credit, including confirmation. This aspect was not mentioned in the relevant article of UCP 500.

The remaining sections of article 48(h) remain unchanged.

UCP 600 article 38.h: No change.

UCP 600 article 38.i: The last section of article 48(i) (UCP 500) refers to the event where the first beneficiary fails to *supply* documents. This finds mention in the revised article 38(i) of UCP 600.

However, the incidence of *discrepancies* created by the documents presented by the first beneficiary is new. The revised text provides that in the event of discrepancies in substituted documents, first beneficiary must replace on demand or second beneficiary's documents may be used.

UCP 600 article 38.j: No change.

UCP 600 article 38.k: This article is new. UCP 500 left room for the second beneficiary to bypass the transferring bank and thereby deny the first beneficiary the opportunity to substitute his invoice and draft (if any) for those of the second beneficiary. This addition in UCP 600 rectifies the situation. This rule ensures that presentation of documents occurs through the transferring bank and that the second beneficiary does not bypass the transferring bank unless specifically authorised by the transferring bank to do so.

Comments:

UCP 600 article 38.e: Revised article probably over-simplified; the revision appears to leave out details that were available in article 48(d) (UCP 500), which could have been helpful to the uninitiated.

UCP 600 article 38.g: The Drafting Group's opinion was that the more items that were allowed to be changed in a transfer, the more would it dilute the understanding of the issuing bank. Hence, the items that *could* be changed were made quite specific, namely those concerning amounts and dates. As outlined in article 1, this however does not restrict the scope for further modification of the rules.

UCP 600 article 38.k: When there is a 100% transfer of the credit amount and no substitution of documents is envisaged, the necessity of the second beneficiary to present documents to the transferring bank does not arise. The second beneficiary may then present documents direct to the issuing bank, provided certain conditions are fulfilled. *This is not stated in the article* but is discussed in the ICC Document no. 470/977 Rev.3 30 October 2002 titled *Transferable credits and the UCP 500 Commission on Banking Technique and Practice.*

ARTICLE 39: ASSIGNMENT OF PROCEEDS

The fact that a credit is not stated to be transferable shall not affect the right of the beneficiary to assign any proceeds to which it may be or may become entitled under the credit, in accordance with the provisions of applicable law. This article relates only to the assignment of proceeds and not to the assignment of the right to perform under the credit.

Under review:

Article 39

Equivalent article in UCP 500:

Article 49.

Analysis:

No change.

Comments:

None, except that this is probably the *only* article that was never touched or taken up for revision right from the word 'go'.

+++

BIBLIOGRAPHY

Bose, Rupnarayan, *An Introduction to Documentary Credits,*, Macmillan India Ltd., 2006.

Bose, Rupnarayan, *Fundamentals of International Banking*, Macmillan India Limited, 2007.

Collyer, Gary, *The Origins of the UCP Revision,* Coastline Solutions Newsletter, July 2006.

Malmqvist, Ole, *UCP 600: Key issues reconsidered,* DC Insight, Special section: Comments on the latest UCP draft.

Case Studies on Documentary Credits, ICC Publication No. 459.

DC Insight, ICC Publication, July-September 2004.

DC Insight, July-September 2006.

First presentation to the Banking Commission, DCInsight, Jan-March 2004.

ICC Asia Annual Survey Conference Series, 2005.

'ICC clarifies 'original document' language in UCP 500', ICC Comments on 'Original Documents'; Paris, 12 July 1999.

ICC Seminar on Documentary Credits, Bombay, December 1977, Pages 67-68.

International Standard Banking Practice for the Examination of Documents under Documentary Credits, ICC Publication No. 645 and 681, International Chamber of Commerce, Paris, France.

Position Papers I to IV, International Chamber of Commerce, 1 September 1994, Paris, France.

Proceedings of ICC Seminar on Revision of Uniform Customs and Practices for Documentary Credits, October 1983, pp. 9, 32;

Report of Seminar on Documentary Credits and Frauds in International Trade, Bombay, November 1985, p.14.

Report of the ICC Banking Commission Meeting, 24-25 October 2005, Paris, France.

Uniform Customs and Practice for Documentary Credits, ICC Publication No. 600, International Chamber of Commerce, Paris, France, December 2006.

Uniform Customs and Practice for Documentary Credits, ICC Publication No. 500, International Chamber of Commerce, Paris, France, 1993.

When a non-bank issues a letter of credit, ICC Department of Policy and Business Practices, Commission on Banking Technique and Practice, 30 October 2002.

+++

www.ingramcontent.com/pod-product-compliance
Lightning Source LLC
LaVergne TN
LVHW021146160826
845679LV00024B/2073

* 9 7 9 8 8 9 0 2 6 1 8 9 2 *